P9-CEY-797

TRUTH

Randy Alcorn

HARVEST HOUSE PUBLISHERS
EUGENE, OREGON

Cover by Kyler Dougherty

Cover Photos © Dovapi / iStock; Steve Richey / Unsplash

Back cover photo © Angie Hunt

TRUTH

Published by Harvest House Publishers
Eugene, Oregon 97402
www.harvesthousepublishers.com

ISBN 978-0-7369-6747-1 (hardcover)

Library of Congress Cataloging-in-Publication Data
Names: Alcorn, Randy C., author.
Title: Truth / Randy Alcorn.
Description: Eugene, Oregon : Harvest House Publishers, 2017.
Identifiers: LCCN 2016040730 (print) | LCCN 2016042740 (ebook) | ISBN 9780736967471 (hardcover) | ISBN 9780736967488 (ebook)
Subjects: LCSH: Truth—Religious aspects—Christianity—Miscellanea. | Truth—Biblical teaching.
Classification: LCC BT50 .A285 2017 (print) | LCC BT50 (ebook) | DDC 202—dc23 LC record available at https://lccn.loc.gov/2016040730

Printed in China

17 18 19 20 21 22 23 24 25 / RDS-JC / 10 9 8 7 6 5 4 3 2 1

"We should seek the truth
without hesitation;
and, if we refuse it,
we show that we value the esteem of men
more than the search for truth."

Blaise Pascal

To Tony and Martha Cimmarrusti
and Mary Clayton Wood,

Precious friends who love Christ's truth,
live it, and share it with others.

INTRODUCTION
Truth Matters

In *The Fellowship of the Ring*, Bilbo Baggins says to his young cousin, "It's a dangerous business, Frodo, going out your door. You step onto the road, and if you don't keep your feet, there's no knowing where you might be swept off to."

To "keep our feet" in this world requires putting our weight upon what is true.

Theologian J. Gresham Machen wisely said, "Nothing in the world can take the place of truth." Yet we are constantly bombarded with lies that attempt to do just that.

Truth is not something we invent, only something we can discover. God reveals it to us in his Word.

Truth is rooted in the eternal, all-powerful, and unchangeable God. Therefore his promises cannot fail: "Every word of God proves true" (Proverbs 30:5 ESV).

As Christ the living Word is truth, so is his written Word. Though Heaven and Earth will pass away, God's truth never will (Mark 13:31).

Truth is not just something we act upon. It acts upon us. We can't change the truth, but the truth can change us. It sanctifies (sets us apart) from the falsehoods woven into our sin natures.

Jesus prayed, "Sanctify them by the truth; your word is truth" (John 17:17).

Truth in the Bible

A common Old Testament word expressing truth, *emeth*, speaks of a dependable reality that's solid and binding. Truth is the bedrock of human relationships (Exodus 20:16), involving an integrity of thoughts, speech, or actions.

Over half the New Testament uses of *truth*, the Greek word *aletheia*, are in John's Gospel. Truth is reality. What seems to be and what really is are often not the same. As I develop in my novel *Deception*, "Things are not as they appear." To know the truth is to see accurately.

God has written his truth on human hearts, in the conscience (Romans 2:15). If truth is spoken graciously, many are drawn to it, instinctively knowing it will fill the moral vacuum they feel. Every heart longs for truth—even the heart that rejects it.

As followers of Christ, we're to walk in the truth (3 John 3), love the truth, and believe the truth (2 Thessalonians 2:9-12). We're to speak the truth, in contrast to "the cunning and craftiness of people in their deceitful scheming" (Ephesians 4:14). We're to be "speaking the truth in love" (Ephesians 4:15).

Truth is far more than a moral guide, it's inseparable from God's own person. Jesus declared, "I am the way and the truth and the life. No man comes to the Father except through me" (John 14:6). He didn't say he would *show* the truth or *teach* the truth or *model* the truth. He *is* the truth. Truth personified.

That Jesus is the God-man, the second member of the Trinity come in human flesh, is central to our faith. To deny this is to be a "liar" (1 John 2:22). If we get it wrong about Christ, it doesn't matter what else we get right.

The Holy Spirit leads people into truth (John 16:13). We're commanded to know the truth (1 Timothy 4:3), handle the truth accurately (2 Timothy 2:15), and avoid doctrinal untruths (2 Timothy 2:18). Christ's disciples do the truth (John 3:21) and abide in the truth (John 8:31-32). The "belt of truth" holds together our spiritual armor (Ephesians 6:14).

God "does not lie" (Titus 1:2). He is "the God of truth" (Isaiah 65:16 ESV). "God is not human, that he should lie, not a human being, that he should change his mind. Does he speak and then not act? Does he promise and not fulfill?" (Numbers 23:19).

Christ, as the Living Word of God, is inseparable from truth. He not only is the Truth, he is the source of all truth, the embodiment of truth, and therefore the reference point for evaluating all truth-claims.

Those in countries where democratic ideals are embraced might have the illusion they should have a voice when it comes to truth. But the universe is not a democracy.

Truth is not a ballot measure. God does not consult us to determine right and wrong. It's we who must go to revealed Scripture to find out what we should believe. Our culture appeals to whatever now *is*; God appeals to his intentions and design, to what *ought* to be.

When we wonder what's right, we're to turn to God's Word: "For the word of the LORD is right and true" (Psalm 33:4). As Psalm 119 depicts in every one of its 176 verses, God's truth is at the heart of the spiritual life.

Christ the Truth-Teller v. Satan the Liar

Unlike God, the devil promises without delivering. He's always denying, revising, or spinning the truth, rearranging the price tags. Jesus called him a "liar, and the father of lies." He said, "He was a murderer from the beginning, not holding to the truth, for there is no truth in him. When he lies, he speaks his native language" (John 8:44).

Everyone speaks their native language fluently. Have you ever known people who lie so convincingly that it's difficult *not* to believe them? Satan's the best liar in the universe. "Go ahead, you deserve it. This won't hurt anybody." He's articulate, smooth, and persuasive. He murders people, and he lies to cover his murders.

When we speak the truth, we speak Christ's language. When we speak lies, we speak Satan's language. Jesus said, "My sheep listen to my voice" (John 10:27). He says, "But they will never follow a stranger; in fact, they will flee from him because they do not recognize a stranger's voice" (v. 5).

We're to become familiar enough with God's Word that we learn the sound of our Master's voice, and can tell the difference between his voice and the devil's impersonation.

Examining Truth-claims

In an age of endless Internet gossip, tabloids, false advertising, lying politicians, and "made up reality," how important is the truth? Reformer Ulrich Zwingli wrote, "The business of the truth is not to be deserted, even to the sacrifice of our lives."

Luke makes a profound observation: "Now the Berean Jews were of more noble character than those in Thessalonica, for they received the message with great eagerness and examined the Scriptures every day to see if what Paul said was true" (Acts 17:11).

They searched the Scriptures—probing, not just skimming. The Bible should be primary, all other truth-claims secondary. We need a worldview informed and corrected by God's Word.

They searched the Scriptures *daily*. (People died to get the Bible into our hands; the least we can do is read it!) Unless we establish a strong biblical grid, a scriptural filter with which to screen and interpret the world, we'll end up thinking like the world. We desperately need not only

Bible teaching, but group Bible study that explores the text and applies it to daily life.

The test of whether Scripture is my authority is this: Do I allow God's Word to convince me to believe what I don't like, what's contrary to what I've always believed and wanted to believe? Do I believe it even when it offends me?

It's impossible for me to write a book on truth without repeatedly citing God's Word. John Newton said, "He has not promised to reveal new truths, but to enable us to understand what we read in the Bible." Jesus said he would send us the Holy Spirit who "will teach you everything and will remind you of everything I have told you" (John 14:26 NLT).

This book contains reflections not only on the general topic of truth, but also on many facets of truths found in Scripture, including eternity, purity, holiness, and happiness. I hope you'll spend time meditating on the brief reflections, great quotations, and Scriptures. Ask God's Holy Spirit to illuminate your mind as you read.

I always encourage readers to carefully evaluate my words and thoughts in light of Scripture, our objective standard of truth. "This God—his way is perfect; the word of the LORD proves true" (2 Samuel 22:31 ESV).

As you read and contemplate and share these insights with others, may you gain a deeper, more worshipful appreciation for our wonderful Savior Jesus, who is the perfect embodiment of Truth.

TRUTH

DAY 1

Jesus answered, "I am the way and the truth and the life. No one comes to the Father except through me."

John 14:6

Of all truths in the universe, the most important is the truth of who Jesus is. After all, Truth is not merely an impersonal moral standard. It is a living Person who loved us so much he bears on his hands eternal scars because he rescued us.

The phrase "truly I tell you" appears 79 times in Scripture, 78 times spoken by Jesus. He is the Truth, and he tells the truth. We can fully trust everything he says. His promises are written in blood.

"He who believes the truth enters on the enjoyment of a happiness which is of the same nature, and springs from the same sources, as the happiness of God."

John Brown

DAY 2

"You are a king, then!" said Pilate.
Jesus answered, "You say that I am a king. In fact, the reason I was born and came into the world is to testify to the truth. Everyone on the side of truth listens to me."
"What is truth?" retorted Pilate.

John 18:37-38a

What is truth? It is reality. Truth exists whether or not anyone believes it.

When Pilate said of Jesus, "I find no basis for a charge against him" (John 18:38b), he affirmed what he believed and what was indeed true: Jesus was innocent.

Truth-claims are exclusive. Jesus didn't say he was *a* truth, but "*the* truth" (John 14:6). If someone says Jesus isn't the primary truth, then either he's wrong or Jesus is.

"If there is no absolute beyond man's ideas, then there is no final appeal to judge between individuals and groups whose moral judgments conflict. We are merely left with conflicting opinions."

Francis Schaeffer

DAY 3

Jesus said, "Whoever finds their life will lose it, and whoever loses their life for my sake will find it."

MATTHEW 10:39

If we grasp this truth, we'll undergo the ultimate paradigm shift: without Christ, any sacrifice we make is worthless. We are miserable without Jesus. Nothing we have can satisfy us. And even if it did, we couldn't hold on to it.

When we hear Jesus tell us to take up our crosses and follow him, and say we should lose our lives for his sake, we're tempted to think, "Then I will never be happy." But in fact Jesus is saying our short-term sacrifices for him are a means to an end, and that end is true and abundant life: "Whoever loses their life for my sake will *find* it."

"Without the way, there is no going;
without the truth, there is no knowing;
without the life, there is no living."

Thomas à Kempis

DAY 4

The heart is deceitful above all things
and beyond cure.

JEREMIAH 17:9

Scripture is full of disheartening diagnoses, including that the heart is "desperately sick" (ESV).

But the Great Physician must tell us this hard truth so we can say, "Create in me a pure heart, O God" (Psalm 51:10). The Physician also promises, "I will give you a new heart and put a new spirit in you; I will remove from you your heart of stone and give you a heart of flesh. I will put my Spirit in you and move you to follow my decrees" (Ezekiel 36:26-27).

So words that at first sting us deeply don't mean we're without hope, only that we cannot cure ourselves. But God has provided the cure: "Therefore, if anyone is in Christ, the new creation has come: The old has gone, the new is here!" (2 Corinthians 5:17).

"Scripture considers repentance a path
to liberation, not condemnation."

Edward Welch

DAY 5

Jesus prayed, "Now this is eternal life: that they know you, the only true God, and Jesus Christ, whom you have sent."

John 17:3

Eternal life is not found by believing in just any god but by believing in the "only true God." False gods, both religious and secular, litter the landscape. The only true God is the one who sent the only true Savior, Jesus Christ.

Jesus gives us more than eternal existence. He gives us *eternal life:* "But God, being rich in mercy, because of the great love with which he loved us, even when we were dead in our trespasses, made us alive together with Christ—by grace you have been saved—and raised us up with him and seated us with him in the heavenly places in Christ Jesus" (Ephesians 2:4-6 ESV).

This great truth all hinges on the person and work of none other than Jesus Christ.

"We weren't meant to be somebody—we were meant to know Somebody."

John Piper

DAY 6

Every good and perfect gift is from above, coming down from the Father...He chose to give us birth through the word of truth, that we might be a kind of firstfruits of all he created.

JAMES 1:17-18

God's best and most perfect gift to us is Jesus himself: "All things were created through him and for him...and in him all things hold together" (Colossians 1:16-17).

If everything that comes into our lives is Father-filtered, how can we be anything less than optimistic? Our optimism is based squarely on realism: Jesus is real, atonement is real, resurrection is real, Heaven is real, and the gospel really is "good news."

"It is a glorious thing to know that your Father God makes no mistakes in directing or permitting that which crosses the path of your life. It is the glory of God to conceal a matter. It is our glory to trust him, no matter what."

Joni Eareckson Tada

DAY 7

When you were dead in your sins and in the uncircumcision of your flesh, God made you alive with Christ.

COLOSSIANS 2:13

Scripture tells us that apart from Christ, we were "dead in [our] sins." This sounds like bad news since a corpse can't raise itself from the grave.

Salvation is a gift: we contribute absolutely nothing. When Jesus called Lazarus from the tomb, he did the work, not Lazarus. Salvation depends on God's mercy and his faithfulness to his promises.

Faith saves us, and we stay saved because of the sustaining, persevering work of God in our lives. The "good news" includes the fact that we needn't live in fear of losing our salvation: "I give them eternal life, and they shall never perish; no one will snatch them out of my hand" (John 10:28).

"The only thing of our very own which we contribute to our salvation is the sin which makes it necessary."

William Temple

DAY 8

Teach me your way, O Lord,
that I may walk in your truth;
unite my heart to fear your name.

Psalm 86:11 (ESV)

Psalm 86 tells us that we must learn the ways of God in order to walk in the ways of God. Jesus said, "Come to me... Take my yoke upon you and learn from me" (Matthew 11:28-29).

Walk in God's truth, and then you'll be in the position to receive his daily guidance. A.W. Tozer said, "Practice the truth and we may with propriety speak the truth."

Have the courage to ask Christ to show you what *he* really wants for your life—not what others want for you, but what he knows is right for you. Listen to his Word for the answers, and call upon him to show you the truth and empower you to live it.

"If God is your co-pilot, swap seats!"

Max Lucado

DAY 9

Dear friends, let us love one another, for love comes from God. Everyone who loves has been born of God and knows God.

1 John 4:7

God is pleased by our love for each other. It was God, not man, who said it wasn't good for man to be alone (Genesis 2:18). Our source of comfort is the truth that not only will we be with the Lord in Heaven, but also that we'll be with each other. In Heaven, God will delight in his children's love for each other. As we walk and talk and laugh together, he'll take as much pleasure in it as we do.

"Having made us as human beings, [God] respects our humanness and treats us with integrity. That is, he treats us true to the truth of who we are. It is human beings and not God who have made spirituality impractical."

Os Guinness

DAY 10

And the people were shouting, "The voice of a god, and not of a man!" Immediately an angel of the Lord struck him down, because he did not give God the glory, and he was eaten by worms and breathed his last. But the word of God increased and multiplied.

Acts 12:22-24 (ESV)

All human claims to greatness and sovereignty are pretensions. When Herod took credit for godlike powers, he breathed his last, while the God-breathed Word grew.

We can't negotiate God's truth any more than we can negotiate gravity. A crowd, seeing someone jump to escape a skyscraper fire, could vote unanimously to suspend the law of gravity.

What difference would that make?

"Such is the immutability of truth, the patrons of it make it not greater, the opposers make it not less; as the splendour of the sun is not enlarged by them that bless it, nor eclipsed by them that hate it."

Thomas Adams

DAY 11

Whatever is true, whatever is noble, whatever is right, whatever is pure, whatever is lovely, whatever is admirable—if anything is excellent or praiseworthy—think about such things.

PHILIPPIANS 4:8

Each of these qualities in Philippians 4:8 is true of Jesus. To think about these things is to recognize the Source of them and to be determined to give Jesus first place in our lives.

When we see God's goodness and beauty in his creation, it should draw our thoughts and praise to him. Even stopping to smell a flower or pet a dog can be a worshipful experience. We should thank God for these things and learn to see them around us. Then we'll be choosing to view truth in a way that is glorifying to Christ.

"Till you can sing and rejoice and delight in God...you never enjoy the world."

Thomas Traherne

DAY 12

But if you harbor bitter envy and selfish ambition in your hearts, do not boast about it or deny the truth. Such "wisdom" does not come down from heaven but is earthly, unspiritual, demonic.

JAMES 3:14-15

Bitterness is the price we pay for minimizing our sins against God while maximizing others' sins against us. Bitterness denies the truth by making sins against us larger than our sins against God.

The truth of God's grace quenches the smoldering coals of how others have hurt us. When that fire goes out, we are free, because we recognize the meaning of "Forgive us our debts, as we also have forgiven our debtors" (Matthew 6:12).

"Whenever I see myself before God and realize something of what my blessed Lord has done for me at Calvary, I am ready to forgive anybody anything. I cannot withhold it. I do not even want to withhold it."

Martyn Lloyd-Jones

DAY 13

The LORD is good to all;
he has compassion on all he has made.

PSALM 145:9

God's saving grace is experienced by some, but the truth of his common grace is experienced by all. Paul said to unbelievers in Lystra, "In past generations he allowed all the nations to walk in their own ways. Yet he did not leave himself without witness, for he did good by giving you rains from heaven and fruitful seasons, satisfying your hearts with food and gladness" (Acts 14:16-17 ESV).

Jesus has given light to mankind (John 1:9). He is the embodiment of God's love and goodness. He gives people tastes of goodness in sun and rain and food and happiness. May the hearts of people be enabled to attribute those kind secondary provisions to their Primary Source.

"Christ is that ocean in which all true delights and pleasures meet...he is a sea of sweetness without one drop of gall."

John Flavel

DAY 14

For Your faithful love is before my eyes,
and I live by Your truth.

Psalm 26:3 (HCSB)

Do we bow to the authority of God's Word and accept its truths by faith even when it is painful or disturbing to do so? Or does the Bible seem to always agree with us? Do we pridefully believe what we want or humbly believe whatever God has told us?

Many believers seem determined to tone truth down, sand off its hard edges. We're embarrassed by God's truth, afraid it makes him look bad. But God appoints us to deliver his message, not to compose it. He's already done that—it's called the Bible.

God doesn't need editors and PR people. He wants faithful messengers, walking in his truth and showing others how to do the same.

"I plead with God: Purify my perceptions of your truth and transform my feelings so that they are in sync with the truth."

John Piper

DAY 15

Therefore, since we are surrounded by so great a cloud of witnesses, let us also lay aside every weight, and sin which clings so closely, and let us run with endurance the race that is set before us.

Hebrews 12:1 (ESV)

God celebrated Job's character. He was blameless and upright and turned away from evil. Satan claimed Job followed him only because God protected him from harm and failure (Job 1:8-11).

You and I may be subjects of discussion between God and Satan or conversations between God and people in Heaven.

Whether you lie in a rest home or sit alone in your house, you're not alone—an unseen universe watches. And our Savior tells you the truth when he promises he will be with you always no matter how tough this life gets.

"A man's greatest care should be for that place where he dwelleth longest; therefore eternity should be in his scope."

Thomas Manton

DAY 16

Jesus said, "I am the gate; whoever enters through me will be saved."

John 10:9

God loves us enough to tell us the truth. There are two eternal destinations, not one. All roads do not lead to Heaven. Only one does: Jesus Christ.

But even choosing the right eternal path through Jesus is an empowerment of God's grace. In the end, our names are written in Heaven not because we were smart and strong and moral. Rather, "because of him you are in Christ Jesus, who became to us wisdom from God, righteousness and sanctification and redemption" (1 Corinthians 1:30 ESV).

Jesus became for us, and remains for us, what we could never be for ourselves. And that should overwhelm us with thankfulness.

"The founders of every major religion said 'I'll show you how to find God.' Jesus said, 'I am God who has come to find you.'"

Timothy Keller

DAY 17

Opponents must be gently instructed, in the hope that God will grant them repentance leading them to a knowledge of the truth.

2 Timothy 2:25

Once we had no right to come into God's presence. Anyone doing so would have been consumed by the fire of his holiness. But his children have been covered with the righteousness of Christ and transformed by his grace and truth.

That changes everything.

Now God is our Father and we have complete and free access to him. "So let us come boldly to the throne of our gracious God. There we will receive his mercy, and we will find grace to help us when we need it most" (Hebrews 4:16 NLT).

"A true love of God must begin with a delight in his holiness, and not with a delight in any other attribute; for no other attribute is truly lovely without this."

Jonathan Edwards

DAY 18

Even Gentiles, who do not have God's written law, show that they know his law when they instinctively obey it, even without having heard it. They demonstrate that God's law is written in their hearts.

ROMANS 2:14-15 (NLT)

God has written his truth on human hearts. Not all guilt feelings are invalid—they sometimes stem from true moral failure. We do people no favor by saying, "Don't feel guilty," if in fact they are guilty. Our goal should be a conscience cleansed of sin, not merely insensitive to sin.

And that's the beauty of God's plan: grace offers us forgiveness and restoration to relationship with God. And God's grace is every bit as real and true as his law!

"God's answer for your guilt is not to explain it away by circumstances that have victimized you, but to call you to own your sins fully and to entrust them all to Jesus Christ by faith."

Mark Dever

DAY 19

Then Jesus declared, "I am the bread of life. Whoever comes to me will never go hungry, and whoever believes in me will never be thirsty."

John 6:35

We were made for God and we will never be satisfied with less. When my thirst for joy is satisfied by Christ, sin becomes unattractive. I say no to the passing pleasures of sin, not because I don't want pleasure, but because I want a greater and lasting pleasure found only in Christ, the giver of truth. I can either have my thirst quenched in Jesus, or I can plunge deeper into sin in search of what's not there.

When did you last look to God and say something like, "Please, my Savior, help me find in you today all that my heart longs for"?

"No one can live without delight, and that is why a man deprived of spiritual joy goes over to carnal pleasures."

Thomas Aquinas

DAY 20

Jesus said, "Sanctify them by the truth; your word is truth."

John 17:17

When Jesus says to his Father "your word is truth," he is not saying that God's Word contains every truth in the universe, but that everything in it is true. Therefore, what contradicts it is false. C.S. Lewis said, "All that is not eternal is eternally out of date."

Relativism dominates the thinking of most educated people (which means that sometimes uneducated people are morally smarter).

Someone can believe sincerely one plus one is three, but their sincerity has no influence on the truth. There are sincere believers and sincere unbelievers. Sincerity is not the issue. Either God exists or he doesn't. Either the Bible can be trusted or it can't.

"The best evidence of the Bible's being the Word of God is to be found between its covers. It proves itself."

Charles Hodge

DAY 21

The integrity of the upright guides them,
but the crookedness of the treacherous destroys them.

PROVERBS 11:3

A.E. Samaan wrote, "Truth is only relative to those that ignore hard evidence."

A college ethics professor who passionately taught moral relativism was outraged when he discovered over half his class cheated on the final. But weren't they living by his philosophy? Why not give them extra credit?

Why did he get upset when his students acted out the very ethical system he advocated? Because no matter what he claims to believe, he knows that when they cheated, they violated an objective and absolute standard of truthfulness. What they'd done was absolutely wrong. Which confirmed that what he'd taught them was also absolutely wrong.

"Without absolutes revealed from without
by God Himself, we are left rudderless in
a sea of conflicting ideas about matters,
justice and right and wrong, issuing from a
multitude of self-opinionated thinkers."

John Owen

DAY 22

When you received the word of God...you accepted it not as the word of men but as what it really is, the word of God.

1 Thessalonians 2:13 (esv)

In 1523, six years after Martin Luther tacked his 95 theses to the door of the Wittenberg church in Germany, Ulrich Zwingli presented his 67 theses to the Zurich City Council in Switzerland. His first statement was, "All who say that the gospel is invalid without the confirmation of the church err and slander God."

Zurich's civil authorities gave Zwingli permission to do what he would have done even without their permission: continue preaching messages that emphasized the truth of Christ more than the church. He proclaimed, "Christ is the only mediator between God and ourselves."

"For God's sake, do not put yourself at odds with the Word of God. For truly it will persist as surely as the Rhine follows its course. One can perhaps dam it up for a while, but it is impossible to stop it."

Ulrich Zwingli

DAY 23

The creation itself will be liberated from its bondage to decay and brought into the freedom and glory of the children of God.

Romans 8:21

Every time you see or experience something wonderful—a loved one's smile or a rainbow—resolve to thank God for the truth that this fallen world is but a hint of the place he's preparing for us.

Think of all that awaits us on the New Earth because of what our Jesus has done for us. Together with all God's people, we'll have the privilege of celebrating the riches of his kindness to us in that new world of endless adventures.

"Let's not get too settled in, too satisfied with the good things down here on earth. They are only the tinkling sounds of the orchestra warming up. The real song is about to break into a heavenly symphony, and its prelude is only a few moments away."

Joni Eareckson Tada

TRUTH

DAY 24

All your words are true;
all your righteous laws are eternal.

PSALM 119:160

Those who believe Scripture are routinely accused of arrogance. Jesus said God's Word is truth (John 17:17). It's not arrogance to believe what the Bible teaches. It's the opposite. Arrogance is when we believe whatever makes us feel better about ourselves or justifies our actions. We pretend we are qualified to judge truth. Then we end up tailoring truth to fit our preferences.

We are temporary. Our opinions come and go continent to continent, decade to decade, century to century. But God's truth is eternal, never-changing: "Surely the people are grass. The grass withers, the flower fades, but the word of our God will stand forever" (Isaiah 40:7-8 ESV).

"You never know how much you really believe anything until its truth or falsehood becomes a matter of life and death to you...Only a real risk tests the reality of a belief."

C.S. Lewis

DAY 25

If we had forgotten the name of our God
or spread out our hands to a foreign god,
would not God have discovered it,
since he knows the secrets of the heart?

Psalm 44:20-21

God will judge us with complete understanding. Only he knows our innermost intentions and will judge us in light of them: "He will...expose the motives of the heart" (1 Corinthians 4:5). His Word "judges the thoughts and attitudes of the heart" (Hebrews 4:12).

When tempted, our theology becomes cloudy. The truth is, there is no such thing as a private moment. God is never in the dark. We may fool ourselves and others, but never God. He knows what we're thinking about and what we're doing. And it is his appraisal of our life that ultimately matters.

"The fear: If I obey God, I will not be happy. This is the same lie that Satan told in the garden."

Timothy Keller

DAY 26

Jesus said, "Whoever wants to be my disciple must deny themselves and take up their cross and follow me. For whoever wants to save their life will lose it, but whoever loses their life for me and for the gospel will save it."

Mark 8:34-35

It's not always pleasant to talk about and share with others the things God's Word says. When I meditate on it, sometimes Scripture makes me uncomfortable. But my comfort is irrelevant. Being a sold-out follower of Christ, standing up for him, and speaking the truth in love, with grace, is what matters.

"If I profess with the loudest voice and clearest exposition every portion of the truth of God except precisely that little point which the world and the devil are at that moment attacking, I am not confessing Christ, however boldly I may be professing Christ."

Martin Luther

DAY 27

But in keeping with his promise we are looking forward to a new heaven and a new earth, where righteousness dwells.

2 Peter 3:13

The old gospel song, "This world is not my home, I'm just a-passing through," conveys a half-truth. Yes, God's people may pass from the earth to the present Heaven through death, but eventually we'll be back to live forever on the restored Earth.

We are pilgrims in this life, not because our home will never be on Earth, but because our ultimate home isn't on the present Earth (which is under the Curse). But just as the Earth was once our intended home (before sin entered), it will one day again be our home (after sin is removed and the Curse is reversed).

"Life is a journey toward heaven. Why should we labor for anything else, but that which is our proper end and true happiness?"

Jonathan Edwards

DAY 28

The Lord is trustworthy in all he promises
and faithful in all he does.

Psalm 145:13

We ought to expect with the highest confidence only what God has clearly, fundamentally, and absolutely promised. Our expectations should remain within the domain of truth; if we expect God to make our lives easy, our expectations are unbiblical.

Peter tells us, "Dear friends, do not be surprised at the fiery ordeal that has come on you to test you, as though something strange were happening to you. But rejoice inasmuch as you participate in the sufferings of Christ, so that you may be overjoyed when his glory is revealed...those who suffer according to God's will should commit themselves to their faithful Creator and continue to do good" (1 Peter 4:12-13,19).

"God is love, but he also defines what love is. We don't have the license to define love according to our own standards and sensibilities...his standards are the ones that matter."

Francis Chan

DAY 29

Jesus said, "I have told you these things, so that in me you may have peace. In this world you will have trouble. But take heart! I have overcome the world."

John 16:33

Christian pilgrims have the best of both worlds: joy whenever this world reminds us of the next, and solace whenever it doesn't.

God promises us a New Earth, where the worst elements of this world—sorrow, pain, death, and the tears they produce—will be taken away forever (Revelation 21:4). Yet we also know this world's best elements—love, joy, wonder, worship, and beauty—will intensify and be perfected in the remade world.

"Being satisfied in God (or anything) always seems easier when all is going well. But when things you love are being stripped out of your hands, then the test is real. If God remains precious in those moments, then his supreme worth shines more brightly. He is most glorified."

John Piper

DAY 30

Jesus said, "If the world hates you, keep in mind that it hated me first. If you belonged to the world, it would love you as its own. As it is, you do not belong to the world, but I have chosen you out of the world. That is why the world hates you."

John 15:18-19

The world hates Christ-followers because we're connected with him. Jesus tells us, "The world...hates me because I testify that its works are evil" (John 7:7). So the world hates Jesus because he tells the truth about our moral condition of sin and rebellion.

Remaining quiet about these hard truths isn't the way to reach the world for Jesus. Even when it stings us or them, let's humbly tell people what he actually said.

"We must not allow our emotions to hold sway over our minds. Rather, we must seek to let the truth of God rule our minds. Our emotions must become subservient to the truth."

Jerry Bridges

DAY 31

I delight in your decrees;
I will not neglect your word.

Psalm 119:16

Disciples practice disciplines. Spending time with Jesus, by consistently and regularly reading his Word and praying, is an action we control. The choice may sometimes be difficult, but it is not impossible. It is a conscious action that allows us to renew our minds with the truth and to live well.

But instead of fixating on the hard work of spiritual disciplines, focus on the great payoff of delight and finding "great spoil" in God's Word (Psalm 119:162).

Studying God's promises is a treasure hunt resulting in great happiness. Some of the precious gems lie right on the surface; others require digging deeper. When we go to God's Word, the joy of discovery awaits.

"Remember that it is not hasty reading, but serious meditation on holy and heavenly truths, that makes them prove sweet and profitable to the soul."

Thomas Brooks

TRUTH

DAY 32

I consider that our present sufferings are not worth comparing with the glory that will be revealed in us.

Romans 8:18

By the time Paul wrote Romans, he'd endured far more suffering than most of us ever will: beatings, imprisonments, stoning, and more (see 2 Corinthians 11:23-29). Yet like countless believers after him, he could trust God's purpose in his trials.

God uses suffering to purge sin, strengthen commitments, unify believers, produce discernment, foster sensitivity, discipline our minds, impart wisdom, stretch our hope, increase our knowledge of Christ, make us long for truth, lead us to repentance, teach us to give thanks in tough times, increase our faith, and strengthen our character. And once he accomplishes such great things, often we can see the value of our suffering.

"It is not a true gospel that gives us the impression the Christian life is easy, and that there are no problems to be faced."

Martyn Lloyd-Jones

DAY 33

It gave me great joy when some believers came and testified about your faithfulness to the truth, telling how you continue to walk in it. I have no greater joy than to hear that my children are walking in the truth.

3 John 3-4

Lies are unreality. Truth rests upon a reality that for the moment may remain unseen but one day will be seen as overwhelmingly persuasive. The wise person believes God's truth now and lives accordingly, patiently waiting for the day when the truth will be undeniable: "So we fix our eyes not on what is seen, but on what is unseen, since what is seen is temporary, but what is unseen is eternal" (2 Corinthians 4:18).

"The greatest friend of truth is time. Error is always in a hurry, but God's man can afford to await the vindication of time. And if he is not vindicated in his own lifetime, eternity will settle the score."

Vance Havner

DAY 34

See to it that no one takes you captive through hollow and deceptive philosophy, which depends on human tradition and the elemental spiritual forces of this world rather than on Christ.

COLOSSIANS 2:8

Christians who believe biblical truths are skeptical about hundreds of other truth-claims.

Secular society—which we often think of as skeptical—is remarkably gullible about falsehoods they ought to reject.

The Bible is unsympathetic to teachings and worldviews that contradict God's Word: "If anyone teaches otherwise and does not agree to the sound instruction of our Lord Jesus Christ and to godly teaching, they are conceited and understand nothing" (1 Timothy 6:3-4).

Why is false doctrine connected with conceit? A proud person elevates self over God, believing he is smarter than God's Word and can improve on it.

"If false, Christianity is not important. If true, it is of infinite importance. What it cannot be is moderately important."

C.S. Lewis

DAY 35

The law of the LORD is perfect,
refreshing the soul.
The statutes of the LORD are trustworthy,
making wise the simple.

PSALM 19:7

Those who reject God's truth don't believe in nothing; they believe in anything. Once you surrender objective truth, upon what rational basis can you reject even the most absurd truth-claims?

People long to believe in the transcendent—something above and beyond us. That's why UFOs and benevolent aliens fascinate us. We want hope and transcendence without surrender to God and his truths, some of which we find very inconvenient. And some of the same people who believe outrageous stories reject Christianity because they think it's unbelievable!

"It is easier to find a score of men wise enough to discover the truth than to find one intrepid enough, in the face of opposition, to stand up for it."

A.A. Hodge

DAY 36

We demolish arguments and every pretension that sets itself up against the knowledge of God, and we take captive every thought to make it obedient to Christ.

2 Corinthians 10:5

The more we fill our minds with goodness and purity and truth, the greater our resistance to temptation. When wrong thoughts come, we replace them with God's truth, knowing we act not only to the glory of God, but in our own best interests.

Proverbs depicts the man who is seduced into adultery as "an ox going to the slaughter" and like a deer or bird being killed by a hunter (Proverbs 7:21-27).

A believer recovering from sexual addiction told me, "Addicts always think they can get away with it. You won't change until you realize you can't ever get away with it."

"You can't keep the birds from flying over your head, but you can keep them from making a nest in your hair."

Martin Luther

DAY 37

For just as through the disobedience of the one man the many were made sinners, so also through the obedience of the one man the many will be made righteous.

Romans 5:19

The grace and truth of Jesus isn't an add-on or makeover that enhances our lives. Religions can alter behavior. Only Jesus has the power to transform the heart.

In contrast, the modern you-can-have-it-all spirituality is a hodgepodge of biblical truth, undefined beliefs, and modern psychology. It's a church-free, build-it-yourself spirituality that never condemns. Its advocates might speak often of a higher power, sometimes God, but seldom Jesus.

In 2002, Oprah Winfrey said, "Today, whatever it is you believe most deeply, now is the time to embrace it."

Really? Even if you believe in genocide, terrorism, or child abuse? Even if what you believe is utterly false?

"To believe in God is to 'let God be God.' This is the chief business of faith."

Os Guinness

DAY 38

My lips will shout for joy,
when I sing praises to you;
my soul also, which you have redeemed.

Psalm 71:23 (esv)

Christians are often perceived as angry, judgmental people devoid of life's joys. In light of our redemption in Christ, shouldn't we radiate such joy, peace, and contentment that others are naturally drawn to us, wanting what we have?

So why aren't we happier? Unfortunately, many Christians are taught that God doesn't want us happy; he wants us holy. In fact, many Christians labor under the false notion that God himself is not happy. But nothing could be further from the truth!

Let's reject the lie and follow God's truthful admonition: "May the righteous be glad and rejoice before God; may they be *happy* and *joyful*" (Psalm 68:3).

"If you live gladly to make others glad in God, your life will be hard, your risks will be high, and your joy will be full."

John Piper

DAY 39

The LORD is waiting to be merciful to you,
and will rise up to show you compassion.
The LORD is a God of justice;
happy are all who wait for him.

ISAIAH 30:18 (CEB)

God is good. Even if we can't see it today, one day we will.

Those who believe not only in God's love but also his justice will find happiness in trusting and waiting for him to accomplish his plan in the most surprising ways. As we await the day when our faith will be sight, may we live our lives full of the truth and love of our God and King: "Grace, mercy and peace from God the Father and from Jesus Christ, the Father's Son, will be with us in truth and love" (2 John 3).

"Our Lord says to you, 'Peace, child, peace. Relax. Let go. I will catch you. Do you trust me so little?'"

C.S. Lewis

DAY 40

Trust in the Lord with all your heart
and lean not on your own understanding;
in all your ways submit to him,
and he will make your paths straight.

Proverbs 3:5-6

True faith submits to God's plan, whether or not it coincides with ours. We shouldn't pray with faith in our faith, but with faith in the one true God. He welcomes prayers that freely ask, yet trust and submit—instead of demanding and insisting.

Though we're free to ask him to deliver us from difficult circumstances, the final outcome is squarely in God's hands. Proverbs 19:21 (ESV) declares, "Many are the plans in the mind of a man, but it is the purpose of the Lord that will stand."

"Any simpleton can follow the narrow path in the light: faith's rare wisdom enables us to march on in the dark with infallible accuracy, since she places her hand in that of her Great Guide."

Charles Spurgeon

DAY 41

I do not hide your righteousness in my heart;
I speak of your faithfulness and your saving help.
I do not conceal your love and your faithfulness
from the great assembly.

Psalm 40:10

I am all for graciousness and kindness as we speak the truth. I seek to practice this with the non-Christians I'm around. Still, the greatest kindness we can offer them, spoken with humility and faithfulness to the Word, is the good news about Jesus.

That is truth they long for even without knowing it—truth that can transform them and infuse life with meaning and delight.

"'Preach the gospel; use words if necessary'...subtly denigrates the high value that the prophets, Jesus, and Paul put on preaching. Of course, we want our actions to match our words as much as possible. But the gospel is a message, news about an event and a person upon which the history of the planet turns."

Mark Galli

DAY 42

Though outwardly we are wasting away, yet inwardly we are being renewed day by day. For our light and momentary troubles are achieving for us an eternal glory that far outweighs them all.

2 Corinthians 4:16-17

God doesn't merely say that someday we'll get over or forget our light and momentary troubles. He says they're purposeful, not random or useless, based on the truth of God's eternal benefits for us.

If we had no eternal future as resurrected people living with King Jesus, then our present sufferings would be ultimately useless. With Christ's promise, however, no present suffering—regardless of its scope—will prove worthless. Such sufferings are actually a means to an end: incalculable future goodness and everlasting gladness.

"While other worldviews lead us to sit in the midst of life's joys, foreseeing the coming sorrows, Christianity empowers its people to sit in the midst of this world's sorrows, tasting the coming joy."

Timothy Keller

DAY 43

Then we will no longer be infants, tossed back and forth by the waves, and blown here and there by every wind of teaching and by the cunning and craftiness of people in their deceitful scheming.

Ephesians 4:14

What happens when we don't listen to God's truth? We become gullible, believing fairy tales that we came from nothing and are going nowhere, that inanimate objects forever existed, or living things rose from nonliving. Given enough time, the impossible never becomes possible. Scripture warns, "They will turn their ears away from the truth and turn aside to myths" (2 Timothy 4:4).

Theological illiteracy has dramatically increased even among evangelical Christians. Churches desperately need a fresh infusion of true biblical doctrine. Without it, we have nothing to offer a truth-deprived world.

"Doctrine matters. What you believe about God, the gospel, the nature of man, and every major truth addressed in Scripture filters down to every area of your life."

John MacArthur

DAY 44

Man does not live on bread alone but on every word that comes from the mouth of the LORD.

DEUTERONOMY 8:3

We live in the age of dialogue. But when it comes to truth, we need some monologue. Let's shut up for a while and listen to God. When we come to know and love his voice, we will "never follow a stranger" because we "do not recognize a stranger's voice" (John 10:5)

Years ago I stopped listening to talk radio because I didn't like its effects on me. I listen to the Bible instead—and I like what it does to my mind and heart. Scripture and Bible-based audio books and teaching accompany me as I travel. I never regret investing my time this way. Why listen to mere human opinions when you can listen to God?

"The great cause of neglecting the Scriptures is not want of time, but want of heart, some idol taking the place of Christ."

Robert Chapman

DAY 45

If anybody is preaching to you a gospel other than what you accepted, let them be under God's curse!

GALATIANS 1:9

"When tempted, no one should say, 'God is tempting me.' For God cannot be tempted by evil, nor does he tempt anyone." (James 1:13). Similarly, God expects his children not to accommodate ourselves to the evils of our time and culture. We should not redefine what it means to be a Christian in order to conform to current social mores.

We've no credibility as Christians if an ever-changing culture takes the Bible's place as our authority. In every age, some within the churches have taught that the commandments of God are written in pencil. Then they gain comfort and popularity by passing out erasers.

"You are required to believe, to preach, and to teach what the Bible says is true, not what you want the Bible to say is true."

R.C. Sproul

DAY 46

God was reconciling the world to himself in Christ, not counting people's sins against them. And he has committed to us the message of reconciliation. We are therefore Christ's ambassadors, as though God were making his appeal through us...Be reconciled to God.

2 Corinthians 5:19-20

If we truly love people, we won't deny their sin. We will stand next to them as fellow-sinners and share the truth that Jesus died for us all, that nothing we can do warrants his grace, and that all we can do is repent of our sins and gratefully receive his forgiveness.

It's the old description of true evangelism: one beggar telling another beggar where to find bread. They may or may not respond to Jesus. That's not up to us. But we can pray that one day they will embrace the One they long for.

"The truth of the gospel is the principal article of all Christian doctrine."

Martin Luther

DAY 47

As obedient children, do not conform to the evil desires you had when you lived in ignorance. But just as he who called you is holy, so be holy in all you do; for it is written: "Be holy, because I am holy."

1 Peter 1:14-16

For many today, the Christian life is little more than a celebration of cheap grace and pseudo-liberty, with a high tolerance for sin. We need to rediscover an unpopular, yet strangely liberating truth: God is holy and expects us to be holy, by his gracious empowerment. God's grace "teaches us to say 'No' to ungodliness and worldly passions, and to live self-controlled, upright and godly lives in this present age" (Titus 2:12).

"The Spirit's work is...to show us the cross, where the pardon is to be found by the unholy; so that having found the pardon there, we may begin the life of holiness to which we are called."

Horatius Bonar

TRUTH

DAY 48

You make known to me the path of life;
you will fill me with joy in your presence,
with eternal pleasures at your right hand.

Psalm 16:11

People sometimes say, "I'd rather have a good time in Hell than be bored in Heaven."

But the truth is that Hell will be deadly boring—a place where everyone is lonely and miserable, where friendship and good times don't exist. Everything good, enjoyable, fascinating, and exciting comes from God. Without God there will never be anything interesting to do.

The New Heavens and New Earth will be expansive because God is infinitely large. The withered souls of Hell will be infinitely small. There will be no room for pleasure.

"Earth knows ugliness and beauty; it's halfway between heaven and hell. And the inhabitants of earth must decide whether they are to seek the beauty of heaven or the monstrous, unrelieved ugliness of hell."

A.W. Tozer

DAY 49

Now faith is confidence in what we hope for and assurance about what we do not see. This is what the ancients were commended for.

Hebrews 11:1-2

In a world where seeing is believing, people believe much that isn't true. And they disbelieve much that is true. Satan is a master illusionist. We don't see his sleight of hand so we fall for his lies—that what we really want is...sin!

One day we'll see sin as God does. It will be stripped of its illusions and will be utterly and eternally unappealing. May God grant us the grace, by the power of his Spirit and his Word, to help us not to wait until the next life to discover what we should have believed and disbelieved in this one.

"Most of us have become so familiar with sin that we no longer see it as a deadly monster."

Nancy DeMoss Wolgemuth

TRUTH

DAY 50

To the Jews who had believed him, Jesus said, "If you hold to my teaching, you are really my disciples. Then you will know the truth, and the truth will set you free."

JOHN 8:31-32

While we may—with effort and assistance—modify certain behaviors, and even some attitudes, Scripture reminds us we cannot, on our own, alter our fundamental nature. There's hope in Christ, who promises that the truth will set us free. But before moving to freedom, we must come to grips with our bondage apart from Christ.

To be liberated from sin, death, and bondage on the New Earth will not mean we'll enjoy fewer pleasures but far more. And the God who delights in our pleasures will be glorified in our grateful praise.

"There can be no separation from sin till there be union with Christ. The eye of faith looks on mercy and that thaws the heart."

Thomas Watson

DAY 51

Jesus said, "My Father's house has many rooms; if that were not so, would I have told you that I am going there to prepare a place for you?...I will come back and take you to be with me that you also may be where I am."

John 14:2-3

When I travel, I find particular joy in those places that remind me of my lifelong home in Oregon. Likewise, Christian pilgrims find greatest joy in moments when this world reminds them of Heaven—their true home that they've never been to, but their beloved Savior is preparing for them.

A good carpenter envisions, plans, and designs. Then he skillfully works, fashioning his creation. And Jesus isn't just any carpenter—he's a truth-filled, all-knowing, and all-powerful God. The New Earth will be his greatest creative project—handmade for us!

"To come to Thee is to come home from exile...to come to the goal of my desires and the summit of my wishes."

Charles Spurgeon

DAY 52

All Scripture is God-breathed and is useful for teaching, rebuking, correcting and training in righteousness, so that the servant of God may be thoroughly equipped for every good work.

2 Timothy 3:16-17

If I would listen to the voice of the Spirit, I should "put my ear" to God-breathed Scripture. Where better to go to hear my Shepherd's voice?

A woman in our church self-consciously admitted that before going to sleep each night, she reads her Bible and then hugs it as she falls asleep. "Is that weird?" she asked. It's unusual but not weird. Any father would be moved to hear that his daughter falls asleep with his written words held close to her heart. Surely her Father God treasures such an act of childlike love.

"The vigor of our spiritual life will be in exact proportion to the place held by the Bible in our life and thoughts."

George Müller

DAY 53

You ought to live holy and godly lives as you look forward to the day of God and speed its coming. That day will bring about the destruction of the heavens by fire, and the elements will melt in the heat. But in keeping with his promise we are looking forward to a new heaven and a new earth, where righteousness dwells.

2 Peter 3:11-13

God has hung a sign on this Earth that says, "Condemned: Plans in place for radical restoration, to begin soon. Come back and see!"

Just as we shall be glorified in the resurrection, so the Earth will be glorified as the dwelling place of God and mankind together, a place where truth will finally be at home (Revelation 21:3).

"We are earthlings. We were made to live here...For too long, many evangelical Christians have mistakenly believed that the goal of life is to escape the bounds of earth...heaven is merely the first leg of a journey that is round-trip."

Michael Wittmer

DAY 54

You're going to find that there will be times when people will have no stomach for solid teaching, but will fill up on spiritual junk food—catchy opinions that tickle their fancy. They'll turn their backs on truth and chase mirages.

2 Timothy 4:3-4 (msg)

All of us have a theology. The question is whether it's true or false.

Some pastors and television preachers play fast and loose with truth. Much teaching today is popularity-driven, not truth-driven. But Charles Spurgeon said, "Christ's people must have bold, unflinching lion-like hearts, loving Christ first, and His truth next, and Christ and His truth beyond all the world."

We easily confuse what we *want* to be true with actual truth. C.S. Lewis said he wrote to expound "mere" Christianity, "which is what it is and was what it was long before I was born and whether I like it or not."

"Theology is simply that part of religion that requires brains."

G.K. Chesterton

DAY 55

He will wipe every tear from their eyes. There will be no more death or mourning or crying or pain, for the old order of things has passed away.

REVELATION 21:4

We live in a world filled with suffering and death. But as believers, we know the truth: God is with us and won't forsake us, and one day we'll live on a redeemed Earth, a place full of joy and delight.

Yes, the day hasn't yet come when God will "wipe away every tear." But it will come.

God has secured with his blood our eternal welfare and never-ending happiness. Anticipating the glorious and beautiful realities of the resurrection and the New Earth has breathtaking implications for our present happiness. By God's grace we can frontload that future happiness into our lives right now.

"Teach me the happy art of attending to things temporal with a mind intent on things eternal."

Puritan Prayer

DAY 56

Dear friends, do not be surprised at the fiery ordeal that has come on you to test you, as though something strange were happening to you. But rejoice inasmuch as you participate in the sufferings of Christ, so that you may be overjoyed when his glory is revealed.

1 Peter 4:12-13

God tells us we shouldn't be surprised when we suffer. It's as if he's asking, "Whatever gave you the idea that you weren't supposed to suffer?"

I've often heard that it's not God's will for his children to suffer. Yet God speaks about "those who suffer according to God's will" (1 Peter 4:19).

God's truth is that he will deliver believers from eternal suffering. And he will deliver us through present suffering, though not always from it. Remember that whatever adversity we face, Christ has been there first and promises he will be us then (Matthew 28:20).

"Christ leads me through no darker rooms than he went through before."

Richard Baxter

DAY 57

The Word became flesh and made his dwelling among us. We have seen his glory, the glory of the one and only Son, who came from the Father, full of grace and truth.

JOHN 1:14

Truth, by itself, is quick to post warning signs and guardrails at the top of the cliff. Yet it fails to empower people to drive safely—and neglects to help them when they crash.

Grace, by itself, is quick to post ambulances and paramedics at the bottom of the cliff. But it fails to post warning signs and build guardrails. In so doing, it encourages the very self-destruction it attempts to heal.

Truth without grace degenerates into judgmental legalism. Grace without truth degenerates into deceitful tolerance of sin.

Christ's heart is equally grieved by grace-suppression and truth-suppression, by grace-twisting and truth-twisting. Grace and truth are both necessary. Neither by itself is sufficient.

"Love cannot be cut loose from the truth of God's will. Truth shapes how to show love."

John Piper

DAY 58

Jesus said, "Then the righteous will shine like the sun in the kingdom of their Father. Whoever has ears, let them hear."

MATTHEW 13:43

The universe should see our creative ingenuity, our artistic accomplishments, and see most clearly God in us, his image-bearers. I believe that on the New Earth—where we remain fully human—reading, study, discussion, and all forms of intellectual exploration will only be enhanced.

We should view our gradual losses of physical and mental sharpness in this life as merely temporary. We'll never pass our peaks, for our peaks lie before us in the resurrection. The best is yet to be. It's not a fairy tale but God's truth that tells us we will all live happily ever after.

"When you get to Heaven, you will be astonished to see this and that and the other joy that was prepared for you, because Christ thought of you and provided just what you would most appreciate."

Charles Spurgeon

DAY 59

[My Word] will not return to me empty,
but will accomplish what I desire
and achieve the purpose for which I sent it.

Isaiah 55:11

Aleksandr Solzhenitsyn said in his Nobel Prize acceptance address, "One word of truth outweighs the entire world."

What did he mean? That the truth is bigger than we are. Just as the Berlin Wall finally toppled, the weight of all the world's lies can be toppled by a single truth.

Truth resonates in the human heart. People may resist it, yet it's the truth they need, for it's the truth that sets them free.

We should let our feelings—real as they are—point to our need to let the truth of God's words guide our thinking. The paths to our hearts travel through our minds. Truth matters.

"Once your soul has been enlarged by a truth,
it can never return to its original size."

Blaise Pascal

DAY 60

It is God's will that you should be sanctified: that you should avoid sexual immorality; that each of you should learn to control your own body in a way that is holy and honorable.

1 Thessalonians 4:3-4

Many people are "searching for God's will." But what's the point of seeking God's will in less important things if you're ignoring what he has already commanded you, for instance, to stay away from sexual immorality?

To say that sexual sin is common among professing Christians is true, but to imply that it *has* to be common undermines both the truth of Scripture and the indwelling Holy Spirit's power.

The purity of Christ's disciples sets them apart from pagan culture. The church today needs to rediscover the critical part purity plays in our identity as his spotless bride.

"According to the Bible, the primary way to define sin is not just the doing of bad things, but the making of good things into ultimate things."

Timothy Keller

DAY 61

I want to know Christ—yes, to know the power of his resurrection and participation in his sufferings, becoming like him in his death.

PHILIPPIANS 3:10

A passage about God's compassion contains a remarkable statement: "In all their distress he too was distressed" (Isaiah 63:9). The same root word describes both God's and his people's distress. Though God doesn't share our feelings of helplessness or uncertainty, clearly he intends us to see a similarity between our emotional distress and his.

Knowing the truth that the second member of the Trinity suffered unimaginable torture on the cross should correct any notion that God lacks feelings. In the suffering of Jesus, God himself suffered.

Dietrich Bonhoeffer wrote in a Nazi prison camp, "Only the suffering God can help."

"Though my natural instinct is to wish for a life free from pain, trouble, and adversity, I am learning to welcome anything that makes me conscious of my need for Him."

Nancy DeMoss Wolgemuth

DAY 62

God has said, "Never will I leave you; never will I forsake you."

Hebrews 13:5

None of us seek tragedy or welcome it. But should tragedy strike—or if it has already—we would be wise to let go of our limited perspective and let God prove the truth of his promises.

Perhaps you're familiar with the background of the great hymn, "It Is Well with My Soul." The songwriter, Horatio Spafford, had lost his four daughters at sea and wrote the hymn when he was crossing over the part of the ocean where their ship had sunk. The pain was great, but God's grace rose to the occasion. Despite his heartbreak, Spafford could say without pretense, "It is well with my soul."

Only God can perform such a miracle of grace. And that kind of miracle is available to us all.

"In the school of deep, sanctified affliction, the believer learns his poverty and destitution. Here the Lord is exalted."

Octavius Winslow

DAY 63

Jesus said, "Happy are people who have pure hearts, because they will see God."

MATTHEW 5:8 (CEB)

The best-selling novel *The Five People You Meet in Heaven* portrays a man who dies, goes to Heaven, and meets five people who tell him his life mattered. It sounds good, but the book presents a Heaven without God and without Jesus as the object of saving faith. It portrays a "Heaven" that isn't about God but about us.

Heaven without God would be like a honeymoon without a groom. Teresa of Avila said, "Wherever God is, there is Heaven." The corollary is obvious: Wherever God is not, is Hell. Heaven will simply be a physical extension of God's goodness. To be with God—to know him and his truth, to see him—is the central, irreducible draw of Heaven.

"No man ever saw God and lived. And yet, I shall not live till I see God; and when I have seen him, I shall never die."

John Donne

DAY 64

"...the gospel of the glory of the happy God with which I have been entrusted."

1 Timothy 1:11 (author's translation)

Language scholars and lexicons attest that the Hebrew word *asher* and the Greek word *makarios*, usually translated "blessed," both actually mean "happy." In other words, the translation above isn't something I've made up—the truth is confirmed by many scholars who say things such as this: "The term 'blessed' indicates...*supreme happiness*."

Who doesn't like being with happy people? If God weren't happy, living with him forever couldn't possibly appeal to us. God's happiness has significant implications for whether the gospel will be seen as truly good news. If we view God as an eternally happy God who willingly sacrificed himself to purchase our eternal happiness, we'll realize we can choose both God and happiness, rather than one instead of the other.

"To be 'blessed' is to be happy in a very full and rich sense."

Wayne Grudem

DAY 65

You [Lord] make him happy with the joy of your presence.

Psalm 21:6 (CEB)

I love the idea of spending not only eternity but also my present life accompanied, indwelt, and empowered by a God who understands my desires and can fulfill my dreams of happiness because he is happy.

When Jesus said, "Come and share your master's happiness!" (Matthew 25:23), his message was unmistakably true: (1) *God is happy* and (2) *God wants us to join in his happiness.*

Together with other children of our King, we'll celebrate and be happy *with* and *in* him. Who'd believe that the perfect Father, Son, and Spirit would invite us, mere creatures, to share the benefits of their eternally rich relationship? Yet that's exactly what they've done!

"The people of God ought to be the happiest people in all the wide world! People should be coming to us constantly and asking the source of our joy and delight."

A.W. Tozer

DAY 66

Oh, how I love your law!
I meditate on it all day long.

Psalm 119:97

Much of the modern thinking about meditation demeans rational thought. It's a carryover from Transcendental Meditation. Such meditation involves the repetition of a mantra, a word (sometimes the name of a Hindu god) not thoughtfully pondered but mindlessly repeated in order to stop thinking. The goal isn't to focus on words or meaning; the goal is not to focus at all.

In contrast, meditation in the Bible is always on a real person (God) and real words and meanings from God (those in Scripture). May we join David in praying, "Let the words of my mouth and the meditation of my heart be acceptable in your sight, O Lord, my rock and my redeemer" (Psalm 19:14 esv).

"Give yourself to prayer, to reading and meditation on divine truths: strive to penetrate to the bottom of them and never be content with a superficial knowledge."

David Brainerd

DAY 67

Send out your light and your truth;
let them guide me.
Let them lead me to your holy mountain,
to the place where you live.
There I will go to the altar of God,
to God—the source of all my joy.

Psalm 43:3-4 (NLT)

Suppose your wedding date was on the calendar, and you were eagerly thinking of the person you were going to marry. You wouldn't be an easy target for seduction. Likewise, if you've meditated on the Lord Jesus and the culmination of God's redemptive drama, Heaven and the New Earth, sin is terribly unappealing.

That's why thinking of being with Jesus in Heaven leads inevitably to pursuing holiness. It will affect our activities and ambitions, our recreation and friendships, and the way we spend our money and time.

"Oh, Christian brethren, what is our light affliction
when compared to such an eternity as this?
Shame on us if we murmur and complain and
turn back, with such a heaven before our eyes!"

J.C. Ryle

DAY 68

I will praise you as long as I live,
lifting up my hands to you in prayer.
You satisfy me more than the richest feast.
I will praise you with songs of joy.

Psalm 63:4-5 (NLT)

If I buy into the lie that happiness can be found in wealth, beauty, fame, or any other pursuits besides Christ, I'll waste life chasing the wrong things.

But when I believe the truth that ultimate happiness is found only in God, then I'll turn off the TV and put down my phone. I'll back away from the Internet and video games, open the Word of God and ask his Spirit to speak joy into my life.

It takes effort, but when you find happiness in him, the payoff is huge—not only in the life to come, but right here and right now.

"Indeed, man wishes to be happy even when he so lives as to make happiness impossible."

Augustine

DAY 69

The LORD your God is with you,
the Mighty Warrior who saves.
He will take great delight in you;
in his love he will no longer rebuke you,
but will rejoice over you with singing.

ZEPHANIAH 3:17

The Lord of the cosmos delights in us, picks us up, wipes away our tears, and rejoices over us with singing. Incredible! And absolutely true. Those who claim that God doesn't have emotions aren't seeing what Scripture tells us.

God isn't only our creator; he's our loving parent, giving comfort to his child. What a personal and intimate picture: God composing a love song with us in mind and singing it to us.

And he opened Heaven's doors to us. How could we ever doubt the truth of his love?

"We cannot see any reason in ourselves why the Lord should take pleasure in us...But...as the bridegroom rejoiceth over the bride, so does the Lord rejoice over us."

Charles Spurgeon

DAY 70

Nothing in all creation is hidden from God's sight. Everything is uncovered and laid bare before the eyes of him to whom we must give account.

Hebrews 4:13

If full disclosure of our finances or our sexual thoughts would embarrass us, we should be living differently. Shouldn't we be most concerned about what God thinks, whose standards are much higher and who knows the truth?

Let's live each day with this awareness: "But they will have to give account to him who is ready to judge the living and the dead" (1 Peter 4:5).

His judgment extends to what no one else sees: "God will bring every deed into judgment, including every hidden thing, whether it is good or evil" (Ecclesiastes 12:14).

Sobering truths. Yet God's promise that he is "rich in mercy" (Ephesians 2:4) comforts our hearts as we anticipate that day.

"It ought to be the business of every day to prepare for our last day."

Matthew Henry

DAY 71

Stand firm then, with the belt of truth buckled around your waist, with the breastplate of righteousness in place, and with your feet fitted with the readiness that comes from the gospel of peace.

Ephesians 6:14-15

Some people approach the concept of "allowing God to work through me" as if it were some passive condition whereby God invades you and takes over, automatically causing you to live righteously, bypassing your own will.

Not true. The spiritual life is warfare. To win the fight, you must take on the armor of God and wield the sword of God's Word—his eternal truths.

"Each of us has to decide...We can try to persuade ourselves that evil doesn't exist; live for ourselves and wink at evil...Or we can work on God's side, listen for his orders on strategy against the evil, no matter how horrible it is, and know that he can transform it."

Catherine Marshall

DAY 72

Therefore, if anyone is in Christ, he is a new creation. The old has passed away; behold, the new has come.

2 Corinthians 5:17 (esv)

We often underestimate the life-changing power of conversion and the Holy Spirit's enablement in sanctification. "Let's be real; we're only human." True. Yet God graciously grants us a new identity and empowers imperfect humans to live holy lives.

Jesus said, "It is not the healthy who need a doctor, but the sick. I have not come to call the righteous, but sinners to repentance" (Luke 5:31-32). We need a cure for our sin, one that may require nasty-tasting medicine, painful surgery, and rigorous physical therapy.

To hate suffering is easy; to hate sin is not. But God mercifully gives us consequences to our sins so that we can hate them, repent, and find healing.

"The more afflictions you have been under, the more assistance you have had for this life of holiness."

John Flavel

DAY 73

Therefore, as God's chosen people, holy and dearly loved, clothe yourselves with compassion, kindness, humility, gentleness and patience.

Colossians 3:12

We admire ability, while God admires humility. Humility doesn't come naturally or automatically to us. Our God-given humanity necessitates a process by which we mature and grow in humility, perspective, and faith. If we have faith in Christ, then God has declared us righteous through his death, but God also wants us to become righteous in our hearts and daily lives.

The incredible truth is that God is not only preparing a place for us; he's preparing *us* for that place. He does so through daily living, including our suffering. We often want to skip this growth process and get ushered into eternity without suffering. But that wouldn't accomplish God's highest purpose for us.

"Every good thing in the Christian life grows in the soil of humility. Without humility, every virtue and every grace withers."

John Piper

DAY 74

"But what about you?" [Jesus] asked. "Who do you say I am?" Simon Peter answered, "You are the Messiah, the Son of the living God." Jesus replied, "Blessed are you, Simon...for this was not revealed to you by flesh and blood, but by my Father in heaven."

MATTHEW 16:15-17

Jesus said, "I am the way and the truth and the life. No one comes to the Father except through me" (John 14:6). The early church believed it. The apostles preached it: "Salvation is found in no one else, for there is no other name under heaven...by which we must be saved" (Acts 4:12).

Yet a recent poll of 35,000 showed that "57 percent of evangelical church attenders said they believe many religions can lead to eternal life."

Jesus's question: "Who do you say I am?" (Matthew 16:16) remains the most important ever asked.

"You never will go to heaven unless you are prepared to worship Jesus Christ as God."

Charles Spurgeon

DAY 75

Come and see what God has done,
his awesome deeds for mankind!

PSALM 66:5

Philip invited his friend Nathanael to "come and see" Jesus (John 1:45-46). The best way to "come and see" is to open the Bible and learn about Jesus. If you hold him at a distance, you'll never see the truth of who he is.

Have you come? Have you seen him? If not, brace yourself. Because once you see Jesus as he really is, your worldview, your affections, *everything* will change.

The first UK physician to die of the AIDS virus contracted the disease while conducting medical research in Zimbabwe. Near the end, he couldn't talk and had only enough strength to write the letter *J*.

His wife asked, "Jesus?"

He nodded. Yes, Jesus. In the end, Jesus is what mattered.

"If Jesus Christ be God and died for me, then no sacrifice can be too great for me to make for him."

C.T. Studd

DAY 76

Jesus said, "Do not be afraid of those who kill the body but cannot kill the soul. Rather, be afraid of the One who can destroy both soul and body in hell."

MATTHEW 10:28

The same Jesus who spoke words of tender love also spoke some of the harshest words of condemnation in Scripture. Jesus spoke more about Hell than anyone else in the Bible.

Speaking the truth about Hell is extremely unpopular among nonbelievers and Christians alike. But Jesus didn't try to be popular. He knew the most loving thing to do was to warn people about Hell and to offer them the alternative of eternal life in him.

When we minimize the reality of Hell, we also minimize God's amazing grace that delivers us from it.

"If I never spoke of hell, I should think I had kept back something that was profitable, and should look on myself as an accomplice of the devil."

J.C. Ryle

DAY 77

But his delight is in the law of the L*ORD,*
and on his law he meditates day and night.

Psalm 1:2

The Bible is God speaking to us—he tells us the very words are "God-breathed" (2 Timothy 3:16).

Not only do the words matter, but the particular meaning in the mind of God and the inspired author of the words matters. Meditation ungrounded in careful, rational, biblical interpretation is not smart meditation because it bypasses the actual thoughts of God that are intended to communicate specific truths to us.

If we latch onto a few of those words out of context and then attach our false or random meanings, we can make the Bible appear to say whatever we already think.

"Meditation on the text of the Bible assumes that, through study and interpretation, you already know something about what the text means. You can't reflect on and enjoy what you don't understand."

Timothy Keller

DAY 78

But Joseph said to them, "Don't be afraid. Am I in the place of God? You intended to harm me, but God intended it for good to accomplish what is now being done, the saving of many lives."

Genesis 50:19-20

Joseph's brothers betrayed him. Yet Joseph knew that God used their evil to accomplish good.

Have you ever watched halftime at a football game when the band forms words or pictures in the middle of the field? They look great up in the stands or on television. But from the sidelines they're confusing and meaningless. We see life from the sidelines. As we gain God's truth and perspective, we move higher up.

Often we see only the tapestry's underside—the knots, the snarls, the frays. God sees it all from the topside, which he's weaving into something beautiful. One day we'll see all our sufferings with Heaven's perspective. May God give us faith to see it now.

"We are on the wrong side of the tapestry."

G.K. Chesterton

DAY 79

For if you live according to the flesh, you will die; but if by the Spirit you put to death the misdeeds of the body, you will live.

ROMANS 8:13

Resisting temptation is a gutsy, courageous, stubborn refusal to violate God's law. Repeatedly calling upon Christ for the strength to say no to the world, the flesh, and the devil and to say yes to God instead brings ultimate joy that can be found only in knowing and pleasing God.

Remember that Beatles song where Ringo Starr sang, "All I gotta do is act naturally"?

It's hard to imagine worse advice! The truth is, if you act naturally you're toast.

But if you act *supernaturally*, drawing on the power of the indwelling Christ, you'll enjoy great personal benefits, now and later.

"O blessed Jesus, your love is wonderful!...May your lovingkindness be ever before my eyes to induce me to walk in your truth."

John Fawcett

DAY 80

God raised us up with Christ and seated us with him in the heavenly realms in Christ Jesus, in order that in the coming ages he might show the incomparable riches of his grace.

Ephesians 2:6-7

The word "show" in this passage means to reveal progressively. In Heaven we'll learn new things about God, going ever-deeper in our understanding. Truth is eternal, and we will eternally learn new truth.

We'll never comprehend all there is to know about God. But we're told we should be *always* "growing in the knowledge of God" (Colossians 1:10).

When it comes to God, there will always be more to inquire of, ask about, discuss, explore, and discover. What joy!

"Since God is infinite...and since we are finite creatures who will never equal God's knowledge or be omniscient, we may expect that for all eternity we will...go on learning more about God and about his relationship to his creation."

Wayne Grudem

DAY 81

In every way I showed you that by working hard like this we can help those who are weak. We must remember what the Lord Jesus said, "We are more happy when we give than when we receive."

Acts 20:35 (NLV)

Those who don't enjoy giving believe Satan's lie that giving means parting with happiness. The truth is, by giving and doing things for Jesus now, we'll have joy both now and when we get to Heaven.

Happiness, giving, and service are inextricably linked in Scripture. Jesus told us to reach out to the poor and needy, then said, "You *will be happy* if you do this. They cannot pay you back. You will get your pay when the people who are right with God are raised from the dead" (Luke 14:14 NLV).

"Materialism is the stupid philosophy where everything is invested in what will eventually become nothing."

Mark Dever

DAY 82

"'We must celebrate with a feast, for this son of mine was dead and has now returned to life. He was lost, but now he is found.' So the party began."

Luke 15:23-24 (nlt)

In Christ's parable of the lost son, who is it that runs to his son, embraces him, and forgives him? The father, who represents God. Who orders a feast and fills his home with music and dancing? God.

Why did the father say he had to celebrate and be happy? Because he's true to his nature—his happiness compels celebration. He grieves over sin. But when we repent, he throws a party that all Heaven joins in. All because God is happy, enjoys being happy, and wants us to enjoy happiness too.

"I drank of God's pleasure as out of a river. Oh that all were made partakers of this living water."

George Whitefield

DAY 83

Jesus said to them, "I am the bread of life; whoever comes to me shall not hunger, and whoever believes in me shall never thirst."

John 6:35 (ESV)

After offering himself as the bread of life, Jesus said to people starving for peace, hope, significance, and happiness, "If anyone thirsts, let him come to me and drink. Whoever believes in me, as the Scripture has said, 'Out of his heart will flow rivers of living water'" (John 7:37-38 ESV).

Christ quenches our thirst from the inside. His Holy Spirit indwells us so whatever heartbreaking circumstances we face, rivers of life-giving water will flow from our hearts.

What's the response of hungry and thirsty people to finally having plenty to eat and drink? Profound gratitude and joy!

"How sweet all at once it was for me to be rid of those fruitless joys which I had once feared to lose! You drove them from me, you who are the true, the sovereign joy."

Augustine

DAY 84

They tell how you turned to God from idols to serve the living and true God, and to wait for his Son from heaven, whom he raised from the dead—Jesus, who rescues us from the coming wrath.

1 Thessalonians 1:9-10

Some Christians waffle on the reality of Hell, trying to be nice. But true love tells the truth. Instead of asking why God sends people to Hell, we ought to ask why he would save any of us and send us to Heaven.

When God fashioned Adam and Eve, he could have kept them from temptation and so prevented evil, suffering, and hell-bound humans, dead in their sins. But without the high stakes of humanity's alienation from God, there can be no redemption. Without Hell as an alternative, Heaven loses its wonder.

God is all-knowing, all-wise, all-good, and all-loving. To him, the stakes were worth it, and always will be.

"Hell is truth known too late."

J.C. Ryle

DAY 85

There will be false teachers among you.

2 Peter 2:1

Paul warned the elders of the church in Ephesus, "I know that after my departure fierce wolves will come in among you...and from among your own selves will arise men speaking twisted things, to draw away the disciples after them" (Acts 20:29-30).

These "twisted things" often were not outright denials of the Bible. Rather, they were Scripture reinterpreted to fit the widely accepted beliefs of the culture.

More theological battles have been lost to enemies inside the church than to those outside. The evil one has targeted us for deception. Nothing less than the welfare of God's people is at stake.

"As Christ is the end of the Law and the Gospel and has within himself all the treasures of wisdom and understanding, so also is he the mark at which all heretics aim and direct their arrows."

John Calvin

DAY 86

Jesus answered her, "If you knew the gift of God, and who it is that is saying to you, 'Give me a drink,' you would have asked him, and he would have given you living water."

JOHN 4:10 (ESV)

We can get serious with Jesus only when we realize we can't rescue ourselves. Sin requires a radical solution utterly beyond us—salvation in Christ. Our justification by faith in Christ satisfies the demands of God's holiness by exchanging our sins for Christ's righteousness (see Romans 3:21-26).

The fundamental truth? We cannot do for ourselves what Christ can do for us. Water is not a nice option, an add-on that we can choose or get along without. It's absolutely vital to our survival. Jesus is the Water of Life, and life itself. Without him the only alternative is death.

"Jesus is the God whom we can approach without pride and before whom we can humble ourselves without despair."

Blaise Pascal

DAY 87

For if we have been united with him in a death like his, we will certainly also be united with him in a resurrection like his.

ROMANS 6:5

Of Americans who believe in a resurrection of the dead, two-thirds believe they will not have bodies after the resurrection. But this is self-contradictory. A nonphysical resurrection is like a sunless sunrise. There's no such thing. If we didn't have bodies, there's nothing to resurrect.

When Christians are restricted to wheelchairs or beds, or our bodies begin weakening, let's remind ourselves that the strongest and healthiest we've ever felt is only a hint of what we'll be in our resurrected bodies on the New Earth. This isn't wishful thinking. It's true. It's the explicit promise of God.

"We will not be disembodied spirits in the world to come, but redeemed spirits, in redeemed bodies, in a redeemed universe."

R.A. Torrey

DAY 88

When all kinds of trials and temptations crowd into your lives my brothers, don't resent them as intruders, but welcome them as friends! Realise that they come to test your faith and to produce in you the quality of endurance.

James 1:2-3 (Phillips)

How can we possibly obey this command to welcome difficulties? By trusting that God tells the truth when he says these struggles make us better, increase our endurance, expand our ministry, and prepare us for eternal joy.

If learning to trust God is good for us and God loves us enough to act for our good, why are we surprised when difficulties come?

John Piper says, "Wimpy Christians won't survive the days ahead." Only when we jettison ungrounded faith can we replace it with valid faith in the true God—faith that can pass life's most formidable tests.

"When we grow careless of keeping our souls, God recovers our taste of good things by sharp crosses."

Richard Sibbes

TRUTH

DAY 89

"Is not my word like fire," declares the LORD, "and like a hammer that breaks a rock in pieces?"

JEREMIAH 23:29

The fire of God's truth consumes the fleeting opinions of people. The hammer of truth breaks the porous crumbly stones of people's opinions. God's Word alone is the true rock.

If we beat our fists against the rock of Gibraltar, it's not the rock that will be worse for wear, it's us.

French Reformers known as Huguenots had a saying when they stood up to a powerful church that didn't hold to God's truth: "Hammer away, you hostile hands. Your hammers break. God's anvil stands."

"The truth is not about us. It's not self-determined, it's not an accessory. It's about God. And...we hold to it, not because we want to make a statement about ourselves, but because we want true statements to be made about him. We want his glory."

Joshua Harris

DAY 90

If anyone has material possessions and sees a brother or sister in need but has no pity on them, how can the love of God be in that person? Dear children, let us not love with words or speech but with actions and in truth.

1 John 3:17-18

Laying down our lives for others isn't limited to using our time, money, and possessions to help the needy, but it certainly includes it.

What we do with our money doesn't simply indicate where our heart is. According to Jesus, it determines where our heart goes. If our heart is where our treasure is (Matthew 6:19-21), then when we move our treasure somewhere else, our heart follows. This is a remarkable truth. If I want a greater heart for the poor or world missions, there is an easy solution—give to them, and give substantially.

"You can give without loving, but you cannot love without giving."

Amy Carmichael

DAY 91

Can a man scoop fire into his lap without his clothes being burned?...
So is he who sleeps with another man's wife;
no one who touches her will go unpunished.

PROVERBS 6:27,29

Believe and embrace this truth: purity is always smart; impurity is always stupid. Not sometimes. Every time. You're not an exception. Nor am I. There are no exceptions.

Actions true to God's character are *always* rewarded. Actions that violate his character are *always* punished.

That doesn't mean God necessarily intervenes directly. Moral laws are like the law of gravity. When a careless driver loses control and plunges over a cliff, God doesn't suddenly invent gravity to punish the driver's carelessness. Gravity is already in effect. So are God's moral laws. We ignore them at our peril.

"In seeking after holiness we are not so much seeking after a thing as we are seeking a Person...To run hard after holiness is another way of running hard after God."

Kevin DeYoung

TRUTH

DAY 92

Jesus said to them, "You belong to your father, the devil, and you want to carry out your father's desires. He was a murderer from the beginning, not holding to the truth, for there is no truth in him. When he lies, he speaks his native language, for he is a liar and the father of lies."

John 8:44

Jesus loves us and tells us the truth. Satan hates us and lies to us. One of Satan's oldest tactics is to weave a phony web of secrecy, casting an illusion of privacy over our sinful choices.

He says, "No one is watching. No one will know." But he's lying. Someone *is* watching—the Audience of One. And in time, many will know. We can be forgiven. But we never get away with anything.

"There is no neutral ground in the universe; every square inch, every split second, is claimed by God and counter-claimed by Satan."

C.S. Lewis

DAY 93

[God] has also set eternity in the human heart; yet no one can fathom what God has done from beginning to end.

Ecclesiastes 3:11

Have you ever sensed that the world you were made for was not this one but another? Sometimes that eternity God has put in our hearts is awakened and for a moment we realize who we were meant to be.

We long for a future world of truth, justice, purity, and joy—and a King who will bring it. We therefore can't be happy with the present world of lies, injustice, impurity, and suffering. True joy comes in anticipating and living in light of the world yet to come with that world's King.

"Here we sometimes enter into the doorway of happiness; there we shall go into the presence chamber of the King! Here we look over the hedge and see the flowers in Heaven's garden; there we shall walk between the flower beds of delight."

Charles Spurgeon

DAY 94

I keep asking that the God of our Lord Jesus Christ, the glorious Father, may give you the Spirit of wisdom and revelation, so that you may know him better.

EPHESIANS 1:17

After thirty years of walking with Jesus, Paul made an amazing declaration that shows what our heart's desire should always be: "I want to know Christ" (Philippians 3:10).

The more you know about Jesus, the more grounds you have to love him. The doctrines of the deity and humanity of Christ, with all their implications, are vitally important not only to sound doctrine but also to loving our Savior and Lord by getting to know him better. We are all theologians, either good ones or bad ones. I'd rather be a good one—especially when it comes to knowing the truth about Jesus. Wouldn't you?

"Christianity is so much more than getting your doctrine right, but it is not less."

Kevin DeYoung

DAY 95

Jesus said, "But about that day and hour no one knows, not even the angels in heaven, nor the Son, but only the Father."

Matthew 24:36

Christ's second coming has been anticipated for two thousand years. He'll certainly return, but in his own time, not ours. To presume Christ will come before we die is unwise.

"As no one has power over the wind to contain it, so no one has power over the time of their death" (Ecclesiastes 8:8). Meanwhile, what do we gain if we pretend mortality isn't a fact of life? It's neither morbid nor inappropriate to speak of it—it's an honest recognition of the truth (Hebrews 9:27).

One of the greatest gifts you can bestow on your loved ones is a clear understanding of the gospel's promise, including anticipation of all God's children's reunion in the better world.

"Dying is but getting dressed for God.
Our graves are merely doorways cut in sod."

Calvin Miller

DAY 96

Now listen, you who say, "Today or tomorrow we will go to this or that city, spend a year there, carry on business and make money." Why, you do not even know what will happen tomorrow. What is your life? You are a mist that appears for a little while and then vanishes.

James 4:13-14

Reading the obituaries reminds us how short our time on Earth is. The wise person thinks ahead. The foolish one acts as if there's no eternal tomorrow.

The truth is, Christians get two opportunities to live on Earth. This first one is but a dot. But from that dot extends a line, which is our second opportunity to live, this time on a redeemed Earth. Right now, we all live *in* the dot. But if we're wise, we'll live *for* the line.

"As difficult as it is, we need to be mindful of death. We must make decisions with our day of death in mind."

Francis Chan

DAY 97

From [Christ] the whole body, joined and held together by every supporting ligament, grows and builds itself up in love.

Ephesians 4:16

God wants us to love others. But loving others doesn't mean we avoid the truth (which is why the verse above is preceded by the command to speak the truth in love).

When you love someone, you don't want them to sin, because sin is never in their best interests. Sin brings judgment, and we do not want those we love to fall under the judgment of God, but rather to embrace the forgiving grace he went to the cross to offer them.

Truth faces sin head-on. Grace pays for sin, forgives it, and conquers it. And God's people stand up for each other in saying no to sin's assaults.

"Truth is never to be abandoned in the name of love. But love is not to be deposed in the name of truth."

John MacArthur

DAY 98

Jesus said, "And I will ask the Father, and he will give you another advocate to help you and be with you forever—the Spirit of truth. The world cannot accept him, because it neither sees him nor knows him. But you know him, for he lives with you and will be in you."

John 14:16-17

God never leaves us alone. He sends his Holy Spirit who indwells, empowers, and comforts us. He's also given us his Word and his people, to be used by the Holy Spirit to speak truth to us and to motivate us. May we learn to sense God's Spirit at work in and around us. And when we don't, may we trust that he is there and is at work.

"Advance in the Christian life comes not by the work of the Holy Spirit alone, nor by our work alone, but by our responding to and cooperating with the grace the Holy Spirit initiates and sustains."

Donald Whitney

DAY 99

Your statutes are wonderful;
therefore I obey them.
The unfolding of your words gives light;
it gives understanding to the simple.

Psalm 119:129-130

Psalm 119 has 176 verses, all of which allude to God's Word and most of which celebrate its truth. Meditating on God's Word brings us light, wisdom, and joy.

It's a great mystery that the Bible is an increasingly neglected book. People who check social media, texts, and emails multiple times a day think nothing of going day after day without reading God's Word. That's why we are spiritually starved and lack the discernment to know what's true and what's false.

There is no virtue in having a Bible sit unread on a shelf or a Bible app sit unused on your phone. A Bible does us no good as long as it remains closed.

"If you wish to know God, you must know his Word."

Charles Spurgeon

DAY 100

Make every effort to live in peace with everyone and to be holy; without holiness no one will see the Lord.

Hebrews 12:14

The obstacles to seeing God are daunting. God spoke his truth to Moses, "no one may see me and live" (Exodus 33:20).

Yet Job declared, "After my skin has been destroyed, yet in my flesh I will see God" (Job 19:26). Jesus promised that the pure in heart will see God (Matthew 5:8).

On the New Earth, God's resurrected children "will see his face" (Revelation 22:4). Because we will be fully righteous in Christ and completely sinless, we'll be able to see God and live. It will be the joy by which all other joys will be measured.

"This insatiable desire for God's beauty stokes the fire of the Christian life."

Tony Reinke

DAY 101

Jesus asked her, "Woman, where are they? Has no one condemned you?"
"No one, sir," she said.
"Then neither do I condemn you," Jesus declared. "Go now and leave your life of sin."

John 8:10-11

Jesus could have said, "Go burn for your sins." *Or* "Go and feel free to sin some more."

What he did say was, "Go and sin no more."

Jesus didn't deny the truth that she had sinned. She needed to repent. And change.

Jesus didn't deny grace. He offered it. By forgiving her, he empowered her to leave her old life behind.

There is no grace without truth. And grace is among the greatest of truths.

"We need the hope that we have been justified by the substitutionary atonement of Jesus. And we need the hope of the promise of Romans 8:28, that God will work all things together for good for us, even the fallout from our past sins."

Jon Bloom

DAY 102

The earth is the LORD's, and everything in it,
the world, and all who live in it.

PSALM 24:1

God's Word is emphatic on this truth that he owns everything: "'The silver is mine and the gold is mine,' declares the LORD Almighty" (Haggai 2:8).

God doesn't just own all the world's wealth, he's the one who gives us the gifts and abilities to generate it: "Remember the LORD your God, for it is he who gives you the ability to produce wealth" (Deuteronomy 8:18).

When it comes to money and possessions, let's think like investment managers, always looking for the best place to invest the Owner's money, where the eternal payoff is likely to be greatest (Matthew 6:19-20).

Since God owns it all, shouldn't we regularly ask him, "What do you want me to do with your money and possessions?"

"I have held many things in my hands and I have lost them all. But whatever I have placed in God's hands, that I still possess."

Martin Luther

DAY 103

All of you, clothe yourselves with humility toward one another, because, "God opposes the proud but shows favor to the humble." Humble yourselves, therefore, under God's mighty hand, that he may lift you up in due time.

1 Peter 5:5-6

Humility isn't pretending that we're unworthy because it's the spiritual thing to do; it's recognizing that we're unworthy because it's simply true.

J.C. Ryle warned, "Let us watch against pride in every shape—pride of intellect, pride of wealth, pride of our own goodness."

Pride pushes us away from God; humility draws us toward God. By choosing humility, we agree with God about our true condition and our true need for Christ.

We need Christ today just as much as we did the day we came to faith in him. That's a humbling truth we should never forget.

"We humans must confess, 'I am because he is.' Only God can say, 'I am who I am.'"

Jen Wilkin

DAY 104

Jesus said, "I came that they may have life and have it abundantly."

John 10:10 (esv)

While we're promised happiness in eternity, Christ doesn't want us to wait until we die to experience it. The word translated "abundantly" suggests something profuse in quantity and quality—a surpassingly happy life.

Similarly, Scripture explains this full, satisfying life: "God has given us eternal life, and this life is in his Son" (1 John 5:11). The phrase "eternal life" means far more than living forever—it means being happy forever!

The gospel infuses hope and joy into our current circumstances by acknowledging God's greatness over any crisis we'll face. God is for us, and not even death can separate us from God's love (see Romans 8:31-39). If we really believe these truths, how can we not be happy?

"In him the day-spring from on high has visited the world; and happy are we, forever happy, if that day-star arise in our hearts."

Matthew Henry

DAY 105

See what great love the Father has lavished on us, that we should be called children of God! And that is what we are!

1 John 3:1

Christ's love for us extends to every aspect of our lives, in which he is determined to work even the toughest of our life experiences for our eternal good (Romans 8:28). We can rest in the truth that everything that comes into our lives—yes, even evil and suffering—is filtered through his hands of love.

Charles Spurgeon said, "Remember this, had any other condition been better for you than the one in which you are, divine love would have put you there."

"The only love that won't disappoint you is one that can't change, that can't be lost, that is not based on the ups and downs of life...It is something that not even death can take away from you. God's love is the only thing like that."

Timothy Keller

DAY 106

Jesus said, "Very truly I tell you, whoever hears my word and believes him who sent me has eternal life and will not be judged but has crossed over from death to life."

John 5:24

Spirituality, prayer, faith, and church are nothing without the gospel. To see the difference between self-directed, self-centered spirituality and God-revealed, Christ-purchased salvation is to know the difference between Hell and Heaven.

The gospel doesn't only get us to Heaven—more importantly, and before everything else, it gets us to God. He is the one we desperately need. The good news isn't just deliverance from Hell; it's crossing a vast chasm that separated us from life, beauty, and hope, to begin a relationship with Jesus Christ...the source of all those and infinitely more.

"So the gospel also gives us a new way to live...It frees us from sin's stranglehold on our lives, liberates our conscience, and releases us from living according to the principles of this world."

Neil H. Williams

DAY 107

Since, then, you have been raised with Christ, set your hearts on things above, where Christ is, seated at the right hand of God. Set your minds on things above, not on earthly things.

Colossians 3:1-2

When followers of Christ don't have a clear picture of what's promised in eternity, they think, *I'll just do whatever makes me happy.*

A.W. Tozer wrote, "But if [the church] is wise she will consider that she stands in the valley between the mountain peaks of eternity past and eternity to come...We do well to think of the long tomorrow."

The greatest weakness of the western church today is arguably our failure to take seriously the truth that Heaven is our home. God's people desperately need an eternal perspective—a constant awareness that we aren't living primarily for the here and now but rather for the world to come.

"Let your whole life be a preparation for heaven."

Samuel Annesley

DAY 108

As a father has compassion on his children,
so the LORD has compassion on those who fear him;
for he knows how we are formed,
he remembers that we are dust.

PSALM 103:13-14

Some theologians once argued that God was "without passions." Their motive was to distinguish God from the mood swings and erratic and unstable aspects of human emotions.

Unfortunately, many Christians came to believe that God has *no* emotions. They read passages about God's compassion but don't think of it as real compassion.

It's critical that we know the heart of God. He genuinely loves and cares about us. If we believe the lie that he has no emotions, then we'll never feel his love for us, nor will we experience deep love for him.

"God does something to us as well as for us through the cross. He persuades us that he loves us."

Sinclair Ferguson

DAY 109

Jesus said, "Which of these three do you think was a neighbor to the man who fell into the hands of robbers?" The expert in the law replied, "The one who had mercy on him." Jesus told him, "Go and do likewise."

LUKE 10:36-37

Jesus used the parable of the Good Samaritan to teach us compassion and sacrificial action for the weak and needy. While two religious leaders passed by the poor man who had been stripped and beaten by robbers, the Samaritan had pity and helped. He cared for him, at great inconvenience.

J.D. Greear says, "Being able to articulate the gospel with accuracy is one thing; having its truth captivate your soul is quite another." Although the Samaritan wasn't responsible for the man's injuries, he nevertheless took responsibility to help him however he could. Jesus tells us to do likewise.

"Living for others is really the Christ life after all. Oh, the satisfaction, happiness, and joy one gets out of it."

George Washington Carver

DAY 110

As God has said, "I will live with them and walk among them, and I will be their God, and they will be my people."

2 Corinthians 6:16

A.W. Tozer wrote, "The whole outlook of mankind might be changed if we could all believe that we dwell under a friendly sky and that the God of heaven, though exalted in power and majesty, is eager to be friends with us."

Desire is Heaven's signpost. Every longing for friendship and meaning and truth is a longing for God and his perfect world. Craving better health is a longing for the perfect resurrection bodies we'll have on the New Earth. Every longing for romance is a longing for the ultimate romance with Christ. Every thirst for beauty is a thirst for Christ. Every taste of joy is but a foretaste of a greater and more vibrant joy than can be found on Earth now.

"Ere long the weeping willow shall be exchanged for the palm-branch of victory, and sorrow's dewdrops will be transformed into the pearls of everlasting bliss."

Charles Spurgeon

DAY 111

They were longing for a better country—a heavenly one. Therefore God is not ashamed to be called their God, for he has prepared a city for them.

HEBREWS 11:16

I've spent so many delightful hours snorkeling and taking photos of fish in expansive ocean reefs, it affects my view of aquariums. When I see ocean fish in an aquarium, I enjoy watching them, but I feel as if something's wrong. I keep imagining them in the place they belong. The truth is, these fish weren't made for that glass box; they were made for a great ocean.

I suppose the fish don't know any better, but I wonder if their instincts tell them their true home is elsewhere. I know for sure *our* instincts tell us that we're made for someplace far better.

"Our greatest affliction is not anxiety, or even guilt, but rather homesickness—a nostalgia or ineradicable yearning to be at home with God."

Donald Bloesch

DAY 112

For the grace of God...teaches us to say "No" to ungodliness and worldly passions, and to live self-controlled, upright and godly lives in this present age.

Titus 2:11-12

Grace doesn't mean watering down truth or holiness. Jesus didn't lower the bar; he raised it. "You've heard that it was said, 'Do not commit adultery.' I say don't look at a woman with lust" (see Matthew 5:27-28).

Grace raises the bar, but it also enables us to joyfully jump over that bar.

Any concept of grace that leaves us—or our children—thinking that truth is unimportant is not biblical grace.

Grace doesn't make people despise truth; it makes them love and follow truth. Far from a free pass to sin, grace is a supernatural empowerment *not* to sin.

"Physician of my sin-sick soul,
To thee I bring my case;
My raging malady control,
And heal me by thy grace."

John Newton

DAY 113

Now we see only a reflection as in a mirror; then we shall see face to face. Now I know in part; then I shall know fully, even as I am fully known.

1 Corinthians 13:12

Many assume that people who die young are physically or mentally disabled, sick, blind, who don't have wealth or good friends or jobs or *whatever* (fill in the blank) will never experience a better life.

But the theology underlying those assumptions is fatally flawed. We're presuming that our present Earth, bodies, culture, relationships, and lives are superior to those of the New Earth.

What are we thinking? The truth is we have not passed our peaks...and we never will.

God will one day clear away sin, death, and sorrow as surely as builders clear away debris so they can begin new construction.

Rejoice. The best is yet to come!

"The best we can hope for in this life is a knothole peek at the shining realities ahead. Yet a glimpse is enough."

Joni Eareckson Tada

DAY 114

He also made the stars.

Genesis 1:16

God is said to have created the vast starry host as though it were no big thing—"Oh, and by the way, he also made the stars." Effortless.

When we imagine ourselves as big, the enormity of creation corrects us. But when we think ourselves insignificant, we should remember the truth that we're the chosen favored children of the Creator-King!

"The heavens proclaim the glory of God. The skies display his craftsmanship" (Psalm 19:1 NLT).

"Astronomers now find they have painted themselves into a corner because they have proven, by their own methods, that the world began abruptly in an act of creation to which you can trace the seeds of every star, every planet, every living thing in this cosmos and on the earth...That there are what I [an astronomer and physicist] or anyone would call...supernatural forces at work is now, I think, a scientifically proven fact."

Robert Jastrow

DAY 115

In him we were also chosen, having been predestined according to the plan of him who works out everything in conformity with the purpose of his will, in order that we, who were the first to put our hope in Christ, might be for the praise of his glory.

Ephesians 1:11-12

When we read Scripture we're left with the choice to trust—or not—that God works even in our most difficult circumstances, and that he is with us in those same challenging times.

Thomas Brooks said, "A gracious soul may look through the darkest cloud and see God smiling on him."

When we see God as he truly is, both holy and loving, just and merciful, and always thinking of our eternal good, we can bow to his sovereign plans and trust him.

"People treat God's sovereignty as a matter of controversy, but in Scripture it is a matter of worship."

J.I. Packer

DAY 116

The precepts of the LORD are right,
giving joy to the heart.
The commands of the LORD are
radiant, giving light to the eyes.

PSALM 19:8

One of the things I admire about Charles Spurgeon is that the Bible oozed out of his pores, and he let Scripture be Scripture, rarely twisting it to fit his theology.

Spurgeon didn't try to reconcile the paradoxical doctrines of Scripture, including God's sovereignty and human free will. He wrote, "That God predestines, and that man is responsible, are two things that few can see. They are believed to be inconsistent and contradictory; but they are not...Two truths cannot be contradictory to each other...These two truths, I do not believe, can ever be welded into one upon any human anvil, but one they shall be in eternity."

"Don't believe everything you think. You cannot be trusted to tell yourself the truth. Stay in the Word."

Jerry Bridges

DAY 117

Surely your goodness and love will follow me
all the days of my life,
and I will dwell in the house of the LORD *forever.*

Psalm 23:6

We use the term *eternal life* without thinking what it means. Life is an earthly existence in which we work, rest, play, and relate to others in ways that include using our creative gifts to enrich and enjoy culture. Yet we've reduced eternal life to an off-Earth existence stripped of the defining properties of what we actually know life to be.

Eternal life begins in this world when Christ saves us, not after we die. It means enjoying forever life's finest moments on Earth the way they were intended. Since in Heaven we'll finally experience life at its best, it would be more accurate to call our present existence the *beforelife* rather than call what follows the *afterlife.*

"We shall in the future world see...God everywhere present and governing all things, material as well as spiritual."

Augustine

DAY 118

Let the message of Christ dwell among you richly as you teach and admonish one another with all wisdom through psalms, hymns, and songs from the Spirit, singing to God with gratitude in your hearts.

Colossians 3:16

Left to myself, I don't think straight. I believe the lies that are currently popular. God gives me his truth as a moral compass, a reference point to guide me.

It's not my job to fix the compass so it points the direction I want it to. I must believe the truth as it is, thank God for it, and seek to communicate it graciously to others. I start by believing that he is telling the truth, no matter how controversial that truth may seem in a world that changes "truths" like troupe actors change clothes.

"I would sooner a hundred times over appear to be inconsistent with myself than be inconsistent with the Word of God."

Charles Spurgeon

DAY 119

Wisdom's instruction is to fear the Lord,
and humility comes before honor.

Proverbs 15:33

As a writer, I've asked God to give me wisdom—and discovered that wisdom begins with the humility to say, "There's a great deal I don't understand."

If I began by imagining I could wrap my mind around the topics I've tackled—such as the problem of evil and suffering, money and possessions, the New Earth, and the balance of grace and truth—I would be delusional.

In writing and in all my life, I desperately need God's Holy Spirit to teach me his truth: "Christ has poured out his Spirit on you...his Spirit teaches you about everything, and what he teaches is true, not false. Obey the Spirit's teaching, then, and remain in union with Christ" (1 John 2:27 GNT).

"Humility is nothing but the disappearance of self in the vision that God is all."

Andrew Murray

DAY 120

When your words came, I ate them;
they were my joy and my heart's delight,
for I bear your name, L*ORD* *God Almighty.*

Jeremiah 15:16

We should hunger for God's words and delight in them. But first we must develop a taste for them. We live in an age where mental "junk foods" are thrust upon us constantly on television, radio, online, in social media, and even through superficial conversations.

Let's not be content with empty entertainment and diversions. Let's turn instead to the delicious truths in God's Word that energize, strengthen, sustain, and comfort us.

Scripture confronts sin in our lives, prompts us to obedience, and gives us delight in Christ. We need to go to God's Word, open it, read it, meditate on it, and learn to delight in it. It will make us better, deeper, and happier people.

"If you don't have it in your head, you can't have it in your heart."

Bruce Ware

DAY 121

The sleep of a laborer is sweet,
whether they eat little or much,
but as for the rich, their abundance
permits them no sleep.

Ecclesiastes 5:12

Ecclesiastes captures a profound truth that amounts to this: *the more you have, the more you have to worry about.*

Accumulating earthly treasures out of insecurity does nothing but multiply anxiety because those treasures are so temporary and uncertain. They have a short shelf life, and cannot bear the weight of our trust.

That's the beauty of Jesus's instructions to store up treasures in Heaven (Matthew 6:19-21). Treasures in Heaven are safe and await us when we leave this world. We can't take it with us, but we can send it on ahead.

"The key to liberation from the power of materialism is not an exodus from culture—abandoning Wall Street or leaving the wealth of the nation to others—but the grace of giving...Givers for God disarm the power of money. They invite God's grace to flow through them."

Kent Hughes

DAY 122

All these people were still living by faith when they died. They did not receive the things promised; they only saw them and welcomed them from a distance, admitting that they were foreigners and strangers on earth.

HEBREWS 11:13

Part of what makes us strangers on earth is that our Father and most of our spiritual family live in Heaven. The greatest joy of Heaven will be marrying our bridegroom, Jesus. The next greatest joy will be reuniting with our departed loved ones. The longer the separation, the sweeter the reunion. For Christians, death is never the end of a relationship but only an interruption followed by glorious reunion.

"One of the inferences from laughter in heaven (Luke 6:21) is that it is the result of heavenly reunion...Laughter, happiness, and joy are the emotions of reunion...we shall know exhilaration when we will be reunited with those with whom we have shared a lifetime."

John Gilmore

DAY 123

We know also that the Son of God has come and has given us understanding, so that we may know him who is true. And we are in him who is true by being in his Son Jesus Christ. He is the true God and eternal life.

1 John 5:20

I was raised in a non-Christian home. Despite many friends and activities, life felt empty. Night after night I spent hours gazing through my telescope, wondering whether anything had meaning.

As a teenager, I searched for truth, longing to know what the universe was about, wishing my life could count for something. To my surprise, my search for truth led me to Jesus Christ. Friends and family thought I'd move on. By God's grace I never have. Why would I turn from the ultimate Truth who transformed me and purchased eternal life and joy for me?

"The answer to all your doubts and failures begins here: You are not the answer. He is."

N.D. Wilson

DAY 124

Flee from sexual immorality. All other sins a person commits are outside the body, but whoever sins sexually, sins against their own body.

1 Corinthians 6:18

Those who succumb to sexual temptation don't act in their own self-interest. Rather, they act in what they *imagine* is their self-interest. Had they pursued truth, they'd run from temptation as from a live grenade.

Scripture tells us, "A man who commits adultery has no sense; whoever does so destroys himself" (Proverbs 6:32). It says to the one who sleeps with another man's wife, "no one who touches her will go unpunished" (Proverbs 6:29).

The world tells us sexual sin will make us happy. Both Scripture and human experience show that after the passing pleasures, we're left with emptiness, hurt, and destruction.

Sin isn't just wrong—it's stupid.

"When a serpent comes across your path speaking lies, you should run from it or kill it. You shouldn't sit around for a friendly chat."

Edward Welch

DAY 125

How happy is the man who does not follow the advice of the wicked or take the path of sinners or join a group of mockers! Instead, his delight is in the Lord*'s instruction, and he meditates on it day and night.*

Psalm 1:1-2 (HCSB)

The Hebrew word *asher* means happy, and it is correctly translated as such in the Holman Christian Standard Bible version of Psalm 1:1. Unfortunately *blessed*, which now conveys something more like holiness than happiness, is the common translation.

Wouldn't the truth that God is happy and offers deep, abiding happiness in Christ that begins now and goes on forever attract people to the gospel? Since God calls the gospel the "good news of happiness" (Isaiah 52:7 ESV), surely we shouldn't leave happiness out of it!

"Thy Word is full of promises...May I be made rich in its riches, be strong in its power, be happy in its joy, abide in its sweetness, feast on its preciousness, draw vigour from its manna."

Puritan Prayer

DAY 126

Let us be thankful, and so worship God acceptably with reverence and awe, for our "God is a consuming fire."

Hebrews 12:28-29

In C.S. Lewis's *The Lion, the Witch and the Wardrobe,* Susan asks Mr. and Mrs. Beaver about Aslan the Lion:

"Is he—quite safe? I shall feel rather nervous about meeting a lion."

"That you will dearie, and no mistake," said Mrs. Beaver. "If there's anyone who can appear before Aslan without their knees knocking, they're either braver than most or just plain silly."

"Then he isn't safe?" said Lucy.

"Safe?" said Mr. Beaver. "Who said anything about safe? Of course he isn't safe. But he's good. He's the King, I tell you."

This is sound theology—God can be good without being safe; he can be loving without bowing to our every wish or desire. And so he is.

"He's wild, you know. Not like a tame lion."

C.S. Lewis

DAY 127

And he passed in front of Moses, proclaiming,
"The LORD*, the* LORD*, the compassionate and*
gracious God, slow to anger, abounding in love
and faithfulness, maintaining love to thousands,
and forgiving wickedness, rebellion and sin."

EXODUS 34:6-7

In his classic book *The Knowledge of the Holy*, A.W. Tozer wrote, "What comes into our minds when we think about God is the most important thing about us."

There's little consolation in knowing God is your Creator unless you know what he is like. For a creator could be a lying, miserable, unreasonable, unloving, and downright hateful being. Likewise, there is little consolation in knowing God is your Ruler unless you also know that he is a truth-teller who is your Savior, your Comforter, and your best Friend.

"It is of infinite importance...to know
what kind of being God is. For he is...the
only fountain of our happiness."

Jonathan Edwards

DAY 128

Only fools say in their hearts,
"There is no God."
They are corrupt, and their actions are evil;
not one of them does good!

Psalm 14:1 (nlt)

Why does the fool claim there is no God? The answer is in the last half of Psalm 14:1.

What does our sin nature have to do with denying God? Everything. For if there's no God, we will not have to stand before him in judgment and give an account of our lives or answer for our wrongdoing.

That's the ultimate lie, and people are quick to believe it because it's more comfortable. Most people don't deny God's existence primarily for intellectual reasons, but for reasons of moral avoidance and personal preference.

"The more I study nature, the more I stand amazed at the work of the Creator."

Louis Pasteur

DAY 129

I am torn between the two: I desire to depart and be with Christ, which is better by far; but it is more necessary for you that I remain in the body.

PHILIPPIANS 1:23-24

Just as birth was our ticket to this world, so death is our ticket to the next. It's less of an end than a beginning. If you were told today you would be moved from the slums to a beautiful country estate, you would focus not on the life you were ending but the life you were beginning.

Death isn't the worst that can happen to us; for God's children, death is the doorway that opens to the best that can happen to us. That best will go on forever and will never disappoint.

"It won't be long before your faith will be rewarded with the sight of the One who has promised to be with you to the end."

Nancy DeMoss Wolgemuth

DAY 130

To the one who is victorious, I will give the right to eat from the tree of life, which is in the paradise of God.

Revelation 2:7

Though the Lord exiled us from Eden because of our evil, that place remains forever embedded in our hearts. We feel homesick for Eden. We long for what the first man and woman once enjoyed, a perfect Earth with free and untainted relationships with God and each other. Every effort at human progress has tried, and failed, to regain what we lost in the Fall.

Through our connection with Adam and Eve, we share nostalgia for a life we've never known but always longed for. The New Earth awaits us as a renovated and expanded Eden, one that will never again shrink or be taken from us, since we will never again sin.

"If your hope is anchored in Jesus, the worst-case future scenario for you is resurrection and everlasting life."

Scott Sauls

DAY 131

But one thing I do: forgetting what lies behind and straining forward to what lies ahead, I press on toward the goal for the prize of the upward call of God in Christ Jesus.

Philippians 3:13-14 (ESV)

Heaven's prize motivated Paul to run hard and long. He was unashamedly motivated by the prospect of eternal reward, and acknowledged it frequently (1 Corinthians 9:24-25; 2 Corinthians 4:16-18; 5:9-10; 2 Timothy 4:7-8). "Run in such a way as to get the prize," he said, and on the verge of death he spoke longingly of the crown the Judge would award him in Heaven.

If we really believe we'll live eternally in a realm where Christ is the center, where joy and righteous living will mean happiness for all, why don't we get a head start on Heaven through Christ-centered righteous living now?

"The more I know about the Next World the better I will live in this one."

Greg Laurie

DAY 132

Like newborn babies, crave pure spiritual milk,
so that by it you may grow up in your salvation,
now that you have tasted that the Lord is good.

1 Peter 2:2-3

We are prone to spiritual amnesia. But what can we do to not forget what God has done for us? How can we obey what Scripture tells us?

The key to spiritual memory is reminding ourselves daily, by reading and meditating on the Bible, who God is and what he's done for us, and then carrying that renewed perspective with us throughout the day. We require a daily dose of Scripture to retell ourselves the gospel, to stave off dementia of the spirit.

Just as we can't follow road signs unless we get on the road, we can't successfully follow God unless we take the time to read, hear, and contemplate the truths found in his Word.

"Open your Bible. It is the pilgrim's guide, in which God describes the glory yet to be revealed."

Charles Spurgeon

DAY 133

Jesus said, "I have told you these things, so that in me you may have peace. In this world you will have trouble. But take heart! I have overcome the world."

John 16:33

Christianity may never return to its central public role in western cultures. We may be less powerful in establishing laws and policies, but that doesn't change the truth about God's Word, which is "living and active, sharper than any two-edged sword" (Hebrews 4:12 ESV).

Opposition is nothing new, and historically the church's greatest advances have come at the lowest ebb of its popularity.

"We are not to retaliate like an unbeliever, nor sulk like a child, nor lick our wounds in self-pity like a dog, nor just grin and bear it like a Stoic, still less pretend we enjoy it like a masochist. What then? We are to rejoice as a Christian should and even 'leap for joy' (Luke 6:23)."

John Stott

DAY 134

In the beginning was the Word, and the Word was with God, and the Word was God.

John 1:1

The Bible is the written Word of God. Jesus is the living Word of God, the second person of the Trinity. The living Word is the central figure of the written Word, the main character in God's unfolding drama of redemption.

James Merritt says, "The primary purpose of reading the Bible is not to know the Bible but to know God." Jesus is the Word, the central Truth we are to look for in Scripture. We will continue to "read" him for eternity, but will never finish nor exhaust him, and his depths we will never fully explore.

"The longer you know Christ, and the nearer you come to him, still the more do you see of his glory. Every farther prospect of Christ entertains the mind with a fresh delight. He is as it were a new Christ every day—and yet the same Christ still."

John Flavel

DAY 135

"The word of the Lord endures forever."

1 Peter 1:25

Our belief about the Bible's nature, inerrancy, and authority will inevitably affect our personal time with God. It will largely determine whether we trust God's Word or trust ourselves, whether we view Scripture as a binding decree from our divine Judge, or set ourselves up as Scripture's judges.

If we think our culture has a better grasp on truth than God does, why bother reading the Bible? Why not just take our spiritual and moral guidance from academia, scientists, media, celebrities, or whomever else we wish?

Any claim that fails to recognize God as Creator, Savior, and Judge doesn't pass the truth test. We must put God's Word above all those and consume it daily as an athlete in training consumes the best food to yield the most energy to face today's demands.

"All the cunning of the devil is exercised in trying to tear us away from the Word."

Martin Luther

DAY 136

How priceless is your unfailing love, O God!
People take refuge in the shadow of your wings.
They feast on the abundance of your house;
you give them drink from your river of delights.

Psalm 36:7-8

Believing that Heaven will be boring betrays a heresy—that God is boring. That's nonsense. Our imaginations and our capacity for joy and exhilaration were created by that very God!

Note the underlying assumption: Sin is exciting, righteousness is boring. But the opposite is true. Sin robs us of fulfillment because it yanks us out of God's river of delights.

Sin doesn't make life interesting; it makes life empty. Sin doesn't create adventure; it blunts it. Sin's emptiness inevitably leads to boredom. When there's fulfillment, when there's beauty, when we see God as he truly is—an endless reservoir of fascination—boredom becomes impossible.

"Man's chief end is to glorify God
and enjoy him forever."

Westminster Shorter Catechism

DAY 137

If you spend yourselves in behalf of the hungry and
satisfy the needs of the oppressed,
then your light will rise in the darkness,
and your night will become like the noonday.

Isaiah 58:10

Jesus gave to help the poor (John 13:29). He repeatedly commands us to care for the poor.

God's love for the poor is truth wedded to actions. Whether mentoring young people, mowing a widow's lawn, volunteering for prison ministry, working for racial justice and unity, standing up for unborn children, or giving generously of your time and income to missions or inner-city work—if you do it to honor Jesus, you bring a foretaste of the coming New Earth to this hurting Old Earth.

"What does love look like? It has the hands to help others. It has the feet to hasten to the poor and needy. It has eyes to see misery and want. It has the ears to hear the sighs and sorrows of men."

Augustine

DAY 138

Jesus said, "The Son of Man will send out his angels, and they will weed out of his kingdom everything that causes sin and all who do evil. They will throw them into the blazing furnace, where there will be weeping and gnashing of teeth."

MATTHEW 13:41-42

Jesus loved people enough to tell them the truth. Hell is as real as Heaven (Psalm 11:4-6) and as eternal as Heaven (Matthew 25:46). God wants us to avoid Hell. He paid the ultimate price so we could. Nevertheless, apart from trusting Christ for salvation, any person's eternal future will be Hell.

That's a hard truth, but a truth that should compel us to put our eternity in the hands of Jesus...and share the good news of salvation with all who will listen.

"Think lightly of hell, and you will think lightly of the cross. Think little of the sufferings of lost souls, and you will soon think little of the Savior who delivers you from them."

Charles Spurgeon

DAY 139

I pray that out of his glorious riches he may strengthen you with power through his Spirit in your inner being, so that Christ may dwell in your hearts through faith.

Ephesians 3:16-17

Who we are is rooted in Christ and who he has made us, not in our outward appearance or performance. The most important part of our life is the part only God sees. His deepest concern is about our inner being, including our minds.

First Peter 1:13 says we are responsible for the way we think. We're to take charge of our minds and focus them on what is right and true. And that begins not with our duties and plans but with knowing God himself and experiencing his closeness.

"I want the presence of God himself, or I don't want anything at all to do with religion…I want all that God has or I don't want any."

A.W. Tozer

DAY 140

The grass withers and the flowers fall,
but the word of our God endures forever.

Isaiah 40:8

I once was reluctant to accept biblical teachings that seemed to contradict theological positions I inherited from the church where I came to Christ and the Bible college and seminary I attended. I've found it freeing to remind myself that Scripture is my authority. We should never let a theological system ignore or tinker with Truth to make it fit the system.

Let's not get too comfortable with our theology. Instead, let Scripture say what it says and revise our theology accordingly. May we read Scripture and believe it, stretching our theology to embrace the full breadth of God's revealed truth.

"If, then, I find taught in one place that everything is fore-ordained, that is true; and if I find in another place that man is responsible for all his actions, that is true."

Charles Spurgeon

DAY 141

If we say we have no sin, we deceive ourselves, and the truth is not in us. If we confess our sins, he is faithful and just to forgive us our sins and to cleanse us from all unrighteousness.

1 John 1:8-9 (ESV)

It's easier to be restored to a healthy relationship with God than with any other being. As difficult as this is to grasp, when we do, it's happy-making in the extreme.

God is the holiest being in the universe; his standards are infinitely higher than any creature's. It would be natural to conclude, then, that God would be more prone than anyone else to hold our offenses against us. Yet the opposite is true.

Arms wide open, God invites our confession and repentance, which he always meets with grace and forgiveness. He really *does* love us, and doesn't hold our sins against us once we confess and repent.

"The voice of sin is loud, but the voice of forgiveness is louder."

Dwight L. Moody

DAY 142

But from everlasting to everlasting the LORD's love
is with those who fear him,
and his righteousness with their children's children.

PSALM 103:17

Some people are embittered when their commitment to help others keeps them from living their dreams. Others are simply sad. Life seems to have broken its promises, and some people end up regretting years of unfulfilled plans.

But God is not unjust. He is not uncaring. And this is not our only chance at life on Earth. I believe that the New Earth is where countless missed opportunities from this life will be ours for the asking.

"For three things I thank God every day of my life: thanks that he has vouchsafed me knowledge of his works; deep thanks that he has set in my darkness the lamp of faith; deep, deepest thanks that I have another life to look forward to—a life joyous with light and flowers and heavenly song."

Helen Keller

DAY 143

Guide me in your truth and teach me,
for you are God my Savior,
and my hope is in you all day long.

Psalm 25:5

Theology isn't a dried-up system of intellectual affirmations divorced from passion for God; rather, it's a life-transforming, gospel-centered summary of God's truth we're to gladly embrace.

Our superficial culture clings to the latest news, polls, celebrity opinions, and what's trending on Twitter. Bookstores abound with accounts of after-death experiences and interactions with angelic beings, and supposedly even Christ himself, but make claims contrary and foreign to Scripture. Not all, but many of these books drip with false doctrine.

Sound doctrine is critically important because how we think about God and God's Son is critically important. May God help us learn to think deeply and *accurately* about him.

"Adjust your doctrine—or just minimize doctrine—to attract the world, and in the very process of attracting them, lose the radical truth that alone can set them free."

John Piper

DAY 144

Peter and the other apostles replied:
"We must obey God rather than human beings!"

Acts 5:29

Though the Roman government granted the Sanhedrin their authority, when the religious leaders told the apostles not to preach the gospel, they did so anyway. When told, "We gave you strict orders not to teach in this name," the apostles insisted they must obey God, not human authorities.

Sometimes it seems that the American church's highest value is what Francis Schaeffer called "personal peace and affluence." We want to be accepted by everyone. We don't want to be controversial. Above all, we don't want to suffer.

It's time for Christ-followers to stand up and say, "We must speak and live truth, regardless of the consequences." No matter what direction our earthly country may be going, it is our never-ending heavenly country we should faithfully represent.

"In America today, it is considered worse to judge evil than to do evil."

Os Guinness

DAY 145

Dear friends, do not believe every spirit, but test the spirits to see whether they are from God, because many false prophets have gone out into the world.

1 John 4:1

Christ-followers should believe in miracles but not in every claim to the miraculous. This isn't a contradiction. Rather, it's spiritual discernment and submission to the sound doctrine advocated by the apostles.

"Do not believe every spirit" is critical input. Christians who desire to be spiritual can become susceptible to every spiritual claim. God certainly does miracles but not all claims of the miraculous prove true.

Even real miracles can come from a false source. Jesus warned, "For false christs and false prophets will arise and perform great signs and wonders, so as to lead astray, if possible, even the elect" (Matthew 24:24 ESV).

"Be radical about grace and relentless about truth and resolute about holiness."

Ann Voskamp

DAY 146

All people are like grass, and all their faithfulness
is like the flowers of the field.
The grass withers and the flowers fall,
because the breath of the LORD *blows on them.*

ISAIAH 40:6-7

Many Christians think and act as if there is no eternal life. We major in the momentary and minor in the momentous. God says our life here is but "a mist that appears for a little while and then vanishes" (James 4:14). Understanding this is the key to being wise rather than foolish with the time and opportunities God gives us.

God makes clear that it's not just going to Heaven that matters, but knowing, loving, and faithfully serving Christ here. That's what makes today matter, and what will make it count for eternity.

"Desire that your life count for something great! Long for your life to have eternal significance. Want this! Don't coast through life without a passion."

John Piper

DAY 147

I know what it is to be in need, and I know what it is to have plenty. I have learned the secret of being content in any and every situation, whether well fed or hungry, whether living in plenty or in want.

PHILIPPIANS 4:12

Advertising is seductive and manipulative. It programs us, enlarging our wants. It thrives on instilling discontent. Its goal is to create an illusion of need, to stimulate desire, to make us dissatisfied with what God has already provided. Advertising lies. If we'd think it through, we'd see the truth, but our thinking gets cloudy.

Good stewards of God's money think before they make a purchase. We must consciously reject advertising's claims and counter them with God's Word, which instructs us about what we really do need...and what we really don't.

"The human heart in which God has placed eternity is so huge that all the world is too small to satisfy it."

Herman Bavinck

DAY 148

For the law was given through Moses; grace and truth came through Jesus Christ.

John 1:17

Since Jesus was and is the perfect embodiment of grace and truth, we can't bring glory to Christ by separating the two.

Some parents are all about truth but lack grace. This will dishearten their children. Other parents are all about what they imagine is grace, where truth doesn't matter. They sacrifice their children's welfare by letting them go wherever, do whatever, with whomever, and letting them have everything they want.

Sadly, their children may never recover from this false grace. Kids don't need cool parents. They need parents full of both grace *and* truth.

"Anything that an individual Christian or Christian group does that fails to show the simultaneous balance of the holiness of God and the love of God presents to a watching world not a demonstration of the God who exists but a caricature of the God who exists."

Francis Schaeffer

DAY 149

But sexual immorality and all impurity or covetousness must not even be named among you, as is proper among saints.

Ephesians 5:3 (esv)

God wants the very best for us. According to the Bible, this includes forsaking all sexual sins, heterosexual and homosexual. This means no sex outside of a marriage between a man and a woman.

When biblical marriage isn't an option, God calls us to celibacy, just as he does to lifelong singles and those divorced and widowed. He's not cruel in doing this; it's not only for his glory but for our good.

If a lifetime of purity seems inconceivable to you, commit yourself to purity in twenty-four-hour increments. Today, "run away from sexual sin" (1 Corinthians 6:18 erv). Do you want freedom from the actions and obsessions of lust? Get help. Be wise. Avoid temptation. Go to Christ. Trust his promises. Believe and embrace his truth. Experience the sufficiency of his grace. Draw on his power.

"Christians don't flirt with sexual immorality. They flee from it."

Kevin DeYoung

DAY 150

Jesus said, "But at the beginning of creation God 'made them male and female.' 'For this reason a man will leave his father and mother and be united to his wife, and the two will become one flesh'... Therefore what God has joined together, let no one separate."

MARK 10:6-9

Resentment, boredom, and hurt make marriages vulnerable to Satan's lie about the intrigue of a new person. The answer is not finding a new person but fostering a fresh appreciation of the "old" person.

Date your spouse regularly. Bring your spouse into your world. Pray with and for each other. Talk about your struggles, disappointments, and concerns. *Listen to each other.* (Put down that smartphone.) Don't live two separate lives under one roof.

The truth is, all marriages face difficulties. Christian marriages have supernatural resources to face and overcome them.

"There is no bond on earth so sweet, nor any separation so bitter, as that which occurs in a good marriage."

Martin Luther

DAY 151

I rejoice over Your promise
like one who finds vast treasure.

Psalm 119:162 (HCSB)

Humility means realizing how little we really know (1 Corinthians 13:9-12).

God is honored when we go to his Word to learn more about him and his ways. We're to bow to the wisdom of Scripture, even when its mysteries are hard to wrap our minds around. Humility requires that we not think more highly of ourselves than we ought (Romans 12:3) and that we realize how much we have to learn from God.

When the Ethiopian eunuch was puzzling over Scripture, Philip asked, "Do you understand what you are reading?" (Acts 8:30). Asking God to enlighten us and give us insight from his Word will go a long way.

"God has condescended to become an author, and yet people will not read his writings. There are very few that ever gave this Book of God, the grand charter of salvation, one fair reading through."

George Whitefield

DAY 152

For it is by grace you have been saved, through faith—and this is not from yourselves, it is the gift of God—not by works, so that no one can boast.

Ephesians 2:8-9

If I could earn my salvation by doing the right things, I could just as easily lose it by doing the wrong things. Praise God the truth is something different! I can trust God, rely on him and not live in dread that when I fail to be the person I should, I will lose my relationship with God and my eternity in Heaven with Jesus.

"The only way anyone can ever be saved is by works. God requires that his law be fulfilled. And unless you possess perfect righteousness, you will never be justified. Now the issue is this: By whose works will you be justified? Justification by faith alone means that we're justified by the works of Christ alone."

R.C. Sproul

DAY 153

But God demonstrates his own love for us in this:
While we were still sinners, Christ died for us.

Romans 5:8

We may accept the label "sinner" but feel that we're "good sinners" like Mother Teresa, not "bad sinners" like Joseph Stalin. *We* sin like a well-meaning child who makes mistakes, not like a malicious heartless criminal.

This isn't what God tells us. The truth is, while our sins may be different in degree, they're the same in kind. Denying that truth sets us up for moral disaster.

The proud deny their evil; the humble confess it—and are then flooded with grace overflowing in joy and delight.

"It is quite clear that the forgiveness of sins strikes at the very core of human need and experience. It speaks of guilt gone, remorse removed, depression disappearing and emptiness of life eradicated. What power there is in forgiveness! And it all comes abundantly from the gracious hand of God."

Lewis A. Drummond

DAY 154

For we live by faith, not by sight.

2 Corinthians 5:7

A woman walked away from her marriage—without biblical grounds—because in her words, "The Holy Spirit gave me peace about it." When I tried to point to the truth in Scripture, she said she wasn't going to be "legalistic." She's still going to church, claiming the spiritual high ground, while failing to live by the standards of the same Bible she professes to believe, often reads, and hears taught every Sunday.

She told me, "I've never been so close to God." But is being close to God merely a feeling? Or does it mean trusting in and living by faith in the truth God has revealed to us not subjectively but objectively in his Word? Men guilty of murdering their wives have insisted "I loved her." Their actions disprove their words.

"Faith is to believe what you do not see; the reward of this faith is to see what you believe."

Augustine

DAY 155

Jesus said, "Do not rejoice that the spirits submit to you, but rejoice that your names are written in heaven."

LUKE 10:20

God chose me to be his child, despite my sin and rebellion, which he determined to pay for himself. What incredible truth! Our source of joy is the God of all happiness and our never-ending relationship with him.

Contemplating God's grace makes us hate the sin that sent Jesus to the cross and that brings misery to our lives and to the lives of those we love. It should also make us full of happiness that God wants to be our Father, and that he has made us his children twice-over, by giving us new birth as the work of his Spirit and by adopting us into his family.

"If you want to judge how well a person understands Christianity, find out how much he makes of the thought of being God's child, and having God as his Father."

J.I. Packer

DAY 156

I write these things to you who believe in the name of the Son of God so that you may know that you have eternal life.

1 John 5:13

We shouldn't just cross our fingers and hope that our names are written in "the Lamb's book of life" (Revelation 21:27). It's of paramount importance to make sure we're going to Heaven, not Hell.

The voice that whispers, "There's no hurry; you can always think about it later," is not God's voice, the voice of truth. God's Word says, "Now is the day of salvation" (2 Corinthians 6:2), and "Choose for yourselves this day whom you will serve" (Joshua 24:15).

"The motive for repentance is not only sorrow for sin but also a sense of the mercy of God in Christ. We have zero motivation to repent, unless we see the mercy of God awaiting us. Not the slap of God, but the embrace of God."

Ray Ortlund Jr.

DAY 157

John said, "Produce fruit in keeping with repentance."

Luke 3:8

Let's not believe the lie that we may as well go ahead and sin since God will forgive us anyway. This cheapens God's grace. Repentance comes from feeling the weight of sin and reaching out to Christ to lift it from us. Our short-sightedness about sin, and our tolerance for it, reflects our failure to think about eternity. Thinking of Heaven leads inevitably to pursuing holiness.

When we realize the pleasures that await us in God's presence, we can forgo lesser pleasures now. When we realize the possessions that await us in Heaven, we'll gladly give away possessions on Earth to store up more treasures in Heaven. When we realize the power offered to us as rulers in God's kingdom, a power we'll then handle with humility and benevolence, we can forgo the pursuit of lesser power here.

"Let your practice correspond to your profession."

George Whitefield

DAY 158

For the sake of your name, Lord,
forgive my iniquity, though it is great.

Psalm 25:11

What steps must I take to deal with sin?

First, I need to admit the truth that it really is sin, not just a mistake or a little slip. Jesus died for our sins, not our excuses.

Second, I must confess my sin—not to inform him (he already knows), but to verbally agree that what I've done is, in fact, sin.

Third, as a part of my admission and confession, I must genuinely repent. True confession is an expression of guilt, regret, desire, and intention to change. I've had people tell me they were sorry for adultery, but refuse to quit seeing their partner in adultery. Admission minus confession and repentance equals…nothing.

"Repentance is one of the most positive words in the Christian vocabulary! It refers to turning from a destructive path and moving instead into God's abundant life."

Richard Blackaby

DAY 159

"Where, O death, is your victory?
Where, O death, is your sting?"

1 Corinthians 15:55

Ancient merchants often wrote the words *memento mori*—"I remember death"—in large letters on their accounting books. Philip II of Macedon, father of Alexander the Great, commissioned a servant to stand in his presence daily and say, "Philip, you will die."

In contrast, France's Louis XIV decreed that the word *death* not be uttered in his hearing. Most of us are more like Louis than Philip, denying death and avoiding the thought except when it's forced on us.

That God "will swallow up death forever" is one of Scripture's great truths (Isaiah 25:8). Jesus came to "free those who all their lives were held in slavery by their fear of death" (Hebrews 2:15). What takes away death's sting? Only a relationship with Jesus, who is life (John 14:6).

"Death to the Christian is the funeral of all his sorrows and evils and the resurrection of all his joys."

James H. Aughey

DAY 160

And even if our gospel is veiled, it is veiled to those who are perishing. The god of this age has blinded the minds of unbelievers, so that they cannot see the light of the gospel that displays the glory of Christ, who is the image of God.

2 Corinthians 4:3-4

Satan wants unbelievers to reject Christ without fear, he wants Christians to be unmotivated to share Christ, and he wants God to receive less glory for the radical impact of Christ's redemptive work. Without Christ, people are perishing. Ironically, those who think themselves compassionate for denying Hell, or not telling the truth about it, are effectively luring more people to it.

"There seems to be a kind of conspiracy to forget, or to conceal, where the doctrine of hell comes from. The doctrine of hell is not 'mediaeval priestcraft' for frightening people into giving money to the church: it is Christ's deliberate judgment on sin...We cannot repudiate hell without altogether repudiating Christ."

Dorothy Sayers

DAY 161

I know that my redeemer lives,
and that in the end he will stand on the earth.
And after my skin has been destroyed,
yet in my flesh I will see God.

Job 19:25-26

When Jesus Christ came to Earth, one of the names given to him was Immanuel, which means "God with us." Jesus's ascension to Heaven in his resurrected body demonstrated that the incarnation was permanent. The second member of the triune God will be a human being for all eternity, and we'll know him not only as God but as man.

This has great bearing on where God might choose for him to dwell with us forever. His choice for that is the New Earth (Revelation 21:1-3). Just as Jesus Christ is God incarnate, the New Earth will be Heaven incarnate.

"Do not pity me for my blindness, for the first face I see will be the face of my Lord Jesus."

Fanny Crosby

DAY 162

"Great and marvelous are your deeds,
Lord God Almighty.
Just and true are your ways,
King of the nations."

REVELATION 15:3

The times we live in are in no danger of going down in history as "The Era of Deep Thought." In our world, feelings overshadow thinking and sizzle triumphs over substance.

In this shallow culture, how can we keep from turning into trivial Christians? "Reflect on what I am saying," Paul wrote, "for the Lord will give you insight into all this" (2 Timothy 2:7).

When we invest in understanding God's truths, we become people of depth and substance. If you want depth, you have to behold God's truth often, allowing it to make the crucial sixteen-inch journey from your head to your heart.

"The quality of a Christian's experience depends on the quality of his faith, just as the quality of his faith depends in turn on the quality of his understanding of God's truth."

Os Guinness

DAY 163

They called out in a loud voice, "How long, Sovereign Lord, holy and true, until you judge the inhabitants of the earth and avenge our blood?"

Revelation 6:10

Neither God nor his people will be satisfied until his enemies are judged, our bodies raised, sin and Satan defeated, Earth restored, and Christ exalted over all.

The most commonly quoted Scripture today is "Judge not." But Jesus's full statement is "Judge not, that you be not judged. For with the judgment you pronounce you will be judged, and with the measure you use it will be measured to you" (Matthew 7:1-2 ESV).

We all must make judgments daily, and we're being told not to be prideful hypocrites when we do. We should keep in mind that in the final day God will not stand before us in judgment, we will all stand before him. Truth will prevail.

"That which a man spits against heaven, shall fall back on his own face."

Thomas Adams

DAY 164

And I heard a loud voice from the throne saying, "Look! God's dwelling place is now among the people, and he will dwell with them. They will be his people, and God himself will be with them and be their God."

Revelation 21:3

No one wants to go to a Heaven where they endlessly float on clouds and play harps. No one desires a disembodied existence in a spiritual realm; we desire an embodied life on a righteous Earth—which is exactly what God promises.

The Lord Jesus Christ "will transform our lowly bodies so that they will be like his glorious body" (Philippians 3:20-21). As Jesus rose again and lived in a physical body on Earth, so we too, in bodies like his, will rise again to live on a renewed Earth (see 1 Thessalonians 4:14; 1 John 3:2; Revelation 21:1-3).

"We live in an age when there is a false glare on the things of time and a great mist over the things of eternity."

J.C. Ryle

DAY 165

But because of his great love for us, God, who is rich in mercy, made us alive with Christ even when we were dead in transgressions—it is by grace you have been saved.

Ephesians 2:4-5

We were saved by grace alone and should live each day by grace alone. As Jerry Bridges advised, "Preach the gospel to yourself every day."

A good test of whether you believe the true gospel is if it makes you happy. Doesn't good news by definition always make us happy? God calls the gospel "the good news of happiness" (Isaiah 52:7 ESV) and "good news that will cause great joy" (Luke 2:10).

If the gospel required we do enough good works to be saved (an impossibility), it would not be good news at all but terrible news.

"The religion of Christ is the religion of joy...There is every element of joy—deep, ecstatic, satisfying, sanctifying joy—in the gospel of Christ. The believer in Jesus is essentially a happy man."

Octavius Winslow

DAY 166

Open my eyes that I may see
wonderful things in your law.

Psalm 119:18

My Greek professor, Ed Goodrick, reminded us to let the text speak for itself rather than seeing it through the lens of doctrines we'd been taught. I can still hear him saying, "Better to be at home with your Bible and not your theology than to be at home with your theology and not your Bible."

I like to allow God's Word to surprise me, change my mind, and modify my positions. If I come to God's Word with my shields down, God uses it to grab me, taking me where *he* wants. If the truths of Scripture never change your mind because you've already figured everything out, you're missing the joy of discovery.

"The word of God alone can effectually cheer the heart of any sinner. There is no true or solid peace to be enjoyed in the world except in the way of reposing upon the promises of God."

John Calvin

DAY 167

But there were also false prophets among the people, just as there will be false teachers among you. They will secretly introduce destructive heresies, even denying the sovereign Lord who bought them—bringing swift destruction on themselves. Many will follow their depraved conduct and will bring the way of truth into disrepute.

2 Peter 2:1-2

Jesus said, "Beware of false prophets, who come to you in sheep's clothing but inwardly are ravenous wolves" (Matthew 7:15 ESV). He also promised, "False messiahs and false prophets will appear and perform great signs and wonders to deceive, if possible, even the elect" (Matthew 24:24).

Heresies are deadly destructive, but they're also attractive because of the bits of truth they contain. They're like chocolate-covered rat poison. Without its truth-coating, many believers wouldn't swallow its lies.

False doctrine is a killer of ourselves and others. By God's grace we need to believe God's truth, teach it, and cling to it.

"By mixing a little truth with it, they had made their lie far stronger."

C.S. Lewis

DAY 168

At that moment the curtain of the temple was torn in two from top to bottom. The earth shook, the rocks split and the tombs broke open.

Matthew 27:51-52

The cross is God's answer to the question, "Why don't you do something about evil?" God *did* do something...and what he did was so powerful that it ripped in half, from the top down, the fabric of the universe itself.

Evil and suffering formed the crucible in which God demonstrated his love to humankind. His love comes to us soaked in divine blood. One look at Jesus—at his incarnation and the redemption he accomplished for us—should silence the argument that God has withdrawn to some far corner of the universe where he keeps his hands clean and maintains his distance from human suffering.

"Christians have learned that when there seems to be no other evidence of God's love, they cannot escape the cross."

D.A. Carson

DAY 169

Come and see what God has done,
his awesome deeds for mankind!

Psalm 66:5

The only answer to the problem of evil and suffering is not an argument, it's a person—Jesus Christ.

In this world that's so torn and shattered, yet still offers remnants and glimpses of beauty and greatness, I have a profound and abiding hope and faith for the future. Through inconceivable self-sacrifice, Jesus has touched me deeply, given me a new heart, and utterly transformed my life.

Because he willingly entered this world of evil and suffering and didn't spare himself, but took on the worst of it for my sake and yours, he's earned my trust even for what I can't understand. I and countless others, many of whom have suffered profoundly, have found him to be trustworthy.

"Our little time of suffering is not worthy of
our first night's welcome home to Heaven."

Samuel Rutherford

DAY 170

Speaking the truth in love, we will grow to become in every respect the mature body of him who is the head, that is, Christ.

Ephesians 4:15

I wonder how often I've subconsciously supplied the word *sometimes* when reading Scripture: "Sometimes" meditate on God's Word (instead of "day and night"). "Sometimes" pray (instead of "without ceasing"). "Sometimes" speak the truth in love.

Since God says the truth sets people free, love compels us to speak the truth—perhaps especially when we're least inclined to. Our job is not to help each other *feel* good but to help each other *be* good. The truth, when spoken in love, can liberate.

"It is the best and truest friend who honestly tells us the truth about ourselves even when he knows we shall not like it. False friends are the ones who hide such truth from us and do so in order to remain in our favor."

R.C.H. Lenski

DAY 171

For the word of God is alive and active. Sharper than any double-edged sword, it penetrates even to dividing soul and spirit, joints and marrow; it judges the thoughts and attitudes of the heart.

Hebrews 4:12

Sometimes more can be learned from the passages of Scripture we ignore than those we underline. No wonder C.S. Lewis called God "the Transcendental Interferer." God has this annoying habit of stepping into our lives even when we've pulled in the welcome mat and bolted the door.

But the more we allow ourselves to grapple with unsettling passages, the more we are pierced. It seems our only options are to let Jesus wound us until he accomplishes his will or to stay away from his Word. But no true disciple can be content with that. When we submit to the truth, even when it hurts, we'll ultimately find joy.

"God is not otherwise to be enjoyed than as he is obeyed."

John Howe

DAY 172

Be very careful, then, how you live—not as unwise but as wise, making the most of every opportunity, because the days are evil. Therefore do not be foolish, but understand what the Lord's will is.

Ephesians 5:15-17

The Bible reveals God's will. If you want to live in his will, then fill your heart and mind with his Word. Trust in his empowerment to obey him. Confess and repent when you fail. Do this and you will be living in the will of God!

God's will is more than a duty; it's a joyful opportunity. When you know Christ, when you fellowship with his people, and when you saturate yourself in his Word, knowing God's will becomes less mysterious, and doing his will tends to follow.

Knowing and living by the revealed truth of God will set you free.

"We discover the will of God by a sensitive application of Scripture to our own lives."

Sinclair Ferguson

DAY 173

For the grace of God has appeared that offers salvation to all people.

Titus 2:11

Tolerance is the world's self-righteous grace-substitute. It's often mistaken for grace, even by Christians. Tolerance recognizes neither truth nor sin. Saying "everything's acceptable," it negates or trivializes God's standards and thereby Christ's redemptive work. It denies our need for regeneration and transformation, sabotaging and undermining God's grace.

Some make sinners feel comfortable by never talking about sin, or only one sin, the sin of judgmental intolerance.

If, in the name of tolerance, we fail to point out that Jesus is the only way to the Father, we not only fail the truth, we fail to communicate grace to those headed for a Christless eternity. Hence, in the name of tolerance, we don't love people enough to share the truth with them.

"Tolerance has been embraced at the expense of truth...To allow that everyone and everything is right is to destroy the notion of truth itself."

Alistair Begg

DAY 174

Who is like the LORD our God, the One who sits
enthroned on high,
who stoops down to look on the
heavens and the earth?

PSALM 113:5-6

God created the universe out of nothing. But he doesn't create truthfulness, love, holiness, and happiness as separate entities. Rather, those ever-existing attributes are inherent to his eternal nature.

It's common to hear people say, "I like to think of God not as my judge but as my papa," or "I like to think of Jesus as my friend, not my master." But he's all the things, all the time, that Scripture reveals him to be, including Judge, Father, Friend, and Master. His attributes aren't a breakfast buffet where we choose what we like and leave the rest untouched.

"Would you lose your sorrow? Would you drown your cares? Then go, plunge yourself in the Godhead's deepest sea; be lost in his immensity; and you shall come forth as from a couch of rest, refreshed and invigorated."

Charles Spurgeon

DAY 175

Jesus said, "If you keep my commands, you will remain in my love, just as I have kept my Father's commands and remain in his love."

John 15:10

None of us has diplomatic immunity to the laws of God. We're all under them. No exceptions. The truth is not something we manipulate to further our own ends. It's not something we twist and spin to serve us. We're not masters of the truth; we are servants of the truth. When we break it, it breaks us.

Every time we're tempted to revise or reinterpret or explain away God's truth, we need to take a hard look at ourselves. And more importantly we need to take a long look at God. In fact, Robert Murray M'Cheyne said, "For every look at self, take ten looks at Christ."

"Tolerance is not a spiritual gift; it is the distinguishing mark of postmodernism; and sadly, it has permeated the very fiber of Christianity."

John Stott

DAY 176

"Be still, and know that I am God;
I will be exalted among the nations,
I will be exalted in the earth."

Psalm 46:10

I live by Portland, Oregon, where "Question Authority" bumper stickers capture the predominant worldview. Those who live here often question the highest authority—God. A Gallup poll showed that Portland has a higher percentage of atheists than any large city in America, with San Francisco and Seattle tying for second.

When surrounded by people who don't believe in God and disdain the Bible, it's easy to go with the flow and question whether God's Word is true. But if God is God, then he is the ultimate authority who deserves our trust, not our doubts.

That I can't wrap my brain around everything in God's Word and God's world proves only that I have a very small brain. Fortunately, God understands it all.

"In faith there is enough light for those
who want to believe and enough
shadows to blind those who don't."

Blaise Pascal

DAY 177

Walk with the wise and become wise,
for a companion of fools suffers harm.

PROVERBS 13:20

It's our nature to be influenced by our surroundings. When we put ourselves in a godly atmosphere with godly people, we are influenced toward godliness. When we put ourselves in an ungodly atmosphere with ungodly people, we are influenced toward ungodliness.

God's Word says, "Do not be misled: 'Bad company corrupts good character'" (1 Corinthians 15:33).

The principle is, we become like the people we spend the most time with. God speaks of those who are "lovers of pleasure rather than lovers of God" and warns us, "Have nothing to do with such people" (2 Timothy 3:4-5).

God tells us exactly how to become wise. Walk with—that is, befriend and spend time with—those who are wise.

"Let those be thy choicest companions who have made Christ their chief companion."

Thomas Brooks

DAY 178

Jesus said, "He went to him and bandaged his wounds, pouring on oil and wine. Then he put the man on his own donkey, brought him to an inn and took care of him."

Luke 10:34

Not only are we to share God's truth, we're to show it.

Missionary pioneer William Carey labored to make widow burning illegal in India. Evangelist John Wesley fought slavery. Dwight L. Moody opened homes for underprivileged girls. Charles Spurgeon built seventeen homes to care for elderly women and provided homes for London orphans and a school to educate hundreds of children. Amy Carmichael intervened for the sexually exploited girls of India, building them homes, a school, and a hospital.

We remember these Christians for their evangelism but forget their intervention for the weak, needy, and exploited. Perhaps they were effective in evangelism because *they lived out the gospel they preached.*

"If a commission by an earthly king is considered an honor, how can a commission by a Heavenly King be considered a sacrifice?"

David Livingstone

DAY 179

Do not conform to the pattern of this world, but be transformed by the renewing of your mind. Then you will be able to test and approve what God's will is—his good, pleasing and perfect will.

Romans 12:2

The current tendency to minimize Bible study and sound theology in the interest of focusing on the heart is badly misguided. We need to cultivate our minds in order to instruct and guide our hearts.

Bradley Green wrote, "If in his death Christ redeemed all of who we are, that must include our intellectual life. Christ did not die to redeem part of us, he died to redeem all."

The heart and mind are not enemies. They're both instruments with which we love God. Jesus said, "Love the Lord your God with all your heart and with all your soul and with all your mind" (Matthew 22:37).

"The collision between a Christian mind and a solidly earthbound culture ought to be a violent one."

Harry Blamires

DAY 180

Love must be sincere. Hate what is evil; cling to what is good.

Romans 12:9

This passage presumes we know the difference between good and evil. But in a culture where morals change like fashions, this is increasingly not the case. We must regularly withdraw to Scripture and ask God's Spirit to train our minds and consciences.

We cannot trust the world to shape our view of truth, nor can we trust our hearts, which are deceitful (Jeremiah 17:9). God has given us a new heart in Christ, but we're in the process of sanctification and are still at war with the old nature (Galatians 5:17).

When God tells us what's good and evil, he is both all-knowing, all-wise, and all-good. Despite the contrary voices we hear daily, we can trust him to tell the truth in his Word.

"The ordinary Christian with the Bible in his hand can say that the majority is wrong."

Francis Schaeffer

DAY 181

Brothers and sisters, if someone is caught in a sin, you who live by the Spirit should restore that person gently. But watch yourself, or you also may be tempted.

Galatians 6:1

All Christians are susceptible to sin, including but not limited to sexual sin.

"Pride goes before destruction, a haughty spirit before a fall" (Proverbs 16:18). What level of pride is required to believe that sexual sin could overtake Lot, Samson, David ("a man after God's own heart"), Solomon, the Corinthians, and many Christian leaders today, but not me?

Paul's warnings deserve a prominent place on our mirrors, dashboards, desktops, and computers: "If you think you are standing firm, be careful that you don't fall!" (1 Corinthians 10:12).

"Christ did not die to make good works merely possible or to produce a half-hearted pursuit. He died to produce in us a passion for good deeds. Christian purity is not the mere avoidance of evil, but the pursuit of good."

John Piper

DAY 182

But our God is in the heavens;
He does whatever He pleases.

Psalm 115:3 (NASB)

Our state of mind determines whether the doctrine of God's sovereignty comforts or threatens us. Charles Spurgeon wrote, "There is no attribute of God more comforting to his children than the doctrine of Divine Sovereignty...On the other hand, there is no doctrine more hated by worldlings."

Imagining that God should let us run life our way sets us up to resent God and even lose our faith when our lives don't go as we want. However, that's a faith we should lose—to be replaced with faith in the God of sovereign grace and truth who doesn't keep us from all difficulties but promises to be with us in all difficulties.

"If I had not felt certain that every additional trial was ordered by infinite love and mercy, I could not have survived my accumulated suffering."

Adoniram Judson

DAY 183

And we know that in all things God works for the good of those who love him, who have been called according to his purpose.

Romans 8:28

Fold a paper in half. Then write on the top half the worst things that have happened to you and on the bottom half the best.

Invariably, if enough time has passed since some of those "worst things" happened, then you'll almost certainly find an overlap. Experiences labeled as the worst things *over time* become the reasons behind some of the best things. That's true because God uses the painful, difficult experiences of life for our ultimate good, just as he promises (Romans 8:28).

How is this possible? Because of the awe-inspiring truth that God is both loving and sovereign. Our lists provide persuasive proof that while evil and suffering aren't good, God can use them to accomplish good.

"There is no pit so deep that he is not deeper still."

Betsie ten Boom

DAY 184

Jesus said, "You are the light of the world... let your light shine before others, that they may see your good deeds and glorify your Father in heaven."

MATTHEW 5:14,16

Some Christians have been deceived into thinking that *works* is a dirty word. It's not.

God condemns works done to earn salvation and works done to impress others. But our Lord enthusiastically commends works done through his empowerment and for the right reasons. Immediately after saying our salvation is "not by works," Paul adds: "For we are God's handiwork, created in Christ Jesus to do good works, which God prepared in advance for us to do" (Ephesians 2:10).

God has a lifetime of good works for each of us to do, including many works using our time, money, and possessions for his glory. He will reward us according to whether or not we do them.

"The Christian is a person who makes it easy for others to believe in God."

Robert Murray M'Cheyne

DAY 185

But the L*ORD said to Samuel, "Do not consider his appearance or his height, for I have rejected him. The* L*ORD does not look at the things people look at. People look at the outward appearance, but the* L*ORD looks at the heart."*

1 SAMUEL 16:7

When we judge people by their appearances, often we're dead wrong. We must be careful not to stereotype sainthood. Saints come in many different trappings. We err when we draw too many conclusions from the trappings themselves.

C.S. Lewis said, "There are no ordinary people. You have never talked to a mere mortal...it is immortals whom we joke with, work with, marry, snub and exploit—immortal horrors or everlasting splendors."

It is a fundamental truth of the Christian worldview that things are often not as they appear.

"A man's felicity consists not in the outward and visible blessing of fortune, but in the inward and unseen perfections and riches of the mind."

Thomas Carlyle

DAY 186

Jesus said, "Enter through the narrow gate. For wide is the gate and broad is the road that leads to destruction, and many enter through it. But small is the gate and narrow the road that leads to life, and only a few find it."

MATTHEW 7:13-14

Some people spend far more time preparing for a trip to Disney World than they do preparing for Heaven and considering how they might get there.

The good news is that the small gate that leads to eternal life is not our good works but Christ himself. He said, "I am the gate; whoever enters through me will be saved" (John 10:9). He invites us to enter through him, and he also promises that as we walk the road, he will be with us and in us (Matthew 28:20; John 14:20).

"Jesus is not one of many ways to approach God, nor is he the best of several ways; he is the only way."

A.W. Tozer

DAY 187

Paul said, "I declare to you today that I am innocent of the blood of any of you. For I have not hesitated to proclaim to you the whole will of God."

Acts 20:26-27

God's Word wasn't given to us so we'd gradually abandon and dismiss it piece by piece, leaving the next generation with little to be challenged or transformed by. When we marginalize or refashion truths people once died for, we no longer have truths worth living for.

Some who imagine they "love to hear the Word" are offended when it threatens their comfortable assumptions and lifestyles. Is staying away from certain biblical subjects the solution to avoid a defensive reaction? No! If we're to proclaim "the whole will of God," then our pastors and teachers must teach God's truth even when it's unpopular.

"Help me to see how good Thy will is in all, and even when it crosses mine teach me to be pleased with it."

Puritan Prayer

DAY 188

Jesus prayed, "I have given them the glory that you gave me, that they may be one as we are one—I in them and you in me—so that they may be brought to complete unity. Then the world will know that you sent me and have loved them even as you have loved me."

JOHN 17:22-23

Francis Schaeffer wrote, "Without true Christians loving one another, Christ says the world cannot be expected to listen, even when we give proper answers...the final apologetic which Jesus gives is the observable love of true Christians for true Christians."

Schaeffer knew the importance of truth. But he also understood that the world will believe the gospel is true when it sees the oneness of God's people. We should do all we can to cultivate this unity.

"The disagreement of Christians is the devil's triumph; and what a sad thing is this, that Christians should give Satan cause to triumph."

Thomas Brooks

DAY 189

"Praise and glory and wisdom and thanks and honor and power and strength be to our God for ever and ever. Amen!"

REVELATION 7:12

Most people believe that we'll worship God in Heaven. But many of us don't grasp how thrilling that will be. Multitudes of God's people—from every nation, tribe, people, and language—will gather to praise God for his greatness, wisdom, grace, and mighty work of redemption (Revelation 5:13-14). Overwhelmed by his magnificence, we will bow in unrestrained happiness and worship.

We'll never lose our fascination for God as we get to know him better. We will see God and understand why the angels and living creatures delight to worship him.

"We will constantly be more amazed with God, more in love with God...Our experience of God will never reach its consummation...It will deepen and develop, intensify and amplify, unfold and increase, broaden and balloon."

Sam Storms

DAY 190

Take delight in the LORD,
and he will give you the desires of your heart.

PSALM 37:4

Won't it be wonderful in Heaven to be free from uncertainty about our desires? We often wonder, *Is it good or bad for me to want this thing or that award or his approval or her appreciation?*

Once we become what God has made us to be in Christ, and once we see him fully, we'll see all things—including sin—for what they really are. God won't need to take away our ability to choose; he won't need to restrain us from evil. We will know and never doubt the truth. Sin will have absolutely no appeal to us. Why would it?

"The freedom of heaven, then, is the freedom from sin; not that the believer just happens to be free from sin, but that he is so constituted or reconstituted that he cannot sin. He doesn't want to sin, and he does not want to want to sin."

Paul Helm

DAY 191

Just as people are destined to die once, and after that to face judgment, so Christ was sacrificed once to take away the sins of many; and he will appear a second time, not to bear sin, but to bring salvation to those who are waiting for him.

Hebrews 9:27-28

The old saying "Nothing is certain but death and taxes" is half true. There are tax evaders, but there are no death evaders.

Hebrews 9:27 explains our written-in-stone itinerary: death, then judgment. Scripture says God will judge everyone (Acts 17:31), and he will judge fairly (Genesis 18:25).

The gospel's fantastically good news is that Christ bore our sins, so he can bring us salvation rather than condemnation.

This promise may seem too good, but none of God's promises are too good to be true.

"He may look on death with joy, who can look on forgiveness with faith."

Thomas Watson

TRUTH

DAY 192

Jesus said, "Then the righteous will answer him, 'Lord, when did we see you hungry and feed you?'... The King will reply, 'Truly I tell you, whatever you did for one of the least of these brothers and sisters of mine, you did for me.'"

MATTHEW 25:37,40

Christ made it clear that he takes personally how we treat people, especially his people.

"If you help the poor, you are lending to the LORD—and he will repay you!" (Proverbs 19:17 NLT). The godly should never ignore the poor. What's held against the "goats" in Christ's parable isn't that they did bad to the needy but that they failed to do good to them—a sin of *omission*.

This means we can't wash our hands of responsibility to the poor by saying, "I'm not hurting them." The truth is, we must actively help them.

"The less I spent on myself and the more I gave to others, the fuller of happiness and blessing did my soul become."

Hudson Taylor

DAY 193

Paul and Silas replied, "Believe in the Lord Jesus, and you will be saved—you and your household."

ACTS 16:31

It makes no sense to reject Jesus because some of his followers are hypocrites. Lots of people don't live consistently with beliefs they profess. Christians don't own the monopoly on hypocrisy. The Bible never says that to be saved you have to believe in Christians. It says you have to believe in Jesus.

Sure, there are counterfeit Christians, but the only thing worth counterfeiting is what's valuable. People make counterfeit currency and jewels, not counterfeit bottle caps. Exactly because the truth of the gospel is priceless, we should expect it to be continuously counterfeited.

"I heard one man say that he did not believe there was a true Christian living, because he had found so many hypocrites. I reminded him that there could be no hypocrites if there were no genuine Christians. No one would try to forge bank notes if there were no genuine ones."

Charles Spurgeon

DAY 194

Your word is a lamp for my feet,
a light on my path.

Psalm 119:105

It would be impossible to come to faith in God without the Bible's objective revelation about him, his plan, human sin, sending his Son Jesus to go to the cross and rise again, defeating sin and death. How could we possibly know unless God told us all these truths?

If I am to have any hope and direction as a Christian, it comes down to this: Is the Bible my authority? If so, how much time do I invest in knowing the Word so I can interpret everything else in its light? Or do I give my mind unfiltered access to other things, which then dim Scripture's light and cause me to embrace what's contrary to God's truth?

"It is not enough to believe God is trustworthy...you must hold that whatever proceeds from him is sacred and inviolable truth."

John Calvin

DAY 195

He who was seated on the throne said, "I am making everything new!" Then he said, "Write this down, for these words are trustworthy and true."

Revelation 21:5

After pledging to end all suffering and death and wipe away every tear, Jesus promises to make all things new. "That's my promise," he says, "bought by my blood, permanently inscribed in the scars on my hands and feet."

This is a promise, a precious truth, we can take to the bank. In a world where little seems certain, this is certain!

"My Savior wept that all tears might be wiped from my eyes, groaned that I might have endless song, endured all pain that I might have unfading health, bore a thorned crown that I might have a glory-diadem, bowed his head that I might uplift mine, experienced reproach that I might receive welcome...expired that I might forever live."

Puritan Prayer

DAY 196

But only the redeemed will walk there, and those
the L*ORD* *has rescued will return.*
They will enter Zion with singing; everlasting joy
will crown their heads.
Gladness and joy will overtake them, and
sorrow and sighing will flee away.

ISAIAH 35:9-10

Happiness comes in drawing close to God, the primary source of all happiness. He graciously gives us innumerable secondary sources of happiness. A reconciled relationship with God, in concert with an understanding of the biblical truth of a resurrected Heaven and Earth, assures us of eternal happiness.

The forever that awaits us should color our lives now. We should daily frontload eternity's joys into our present experience. And when we do, people will see "the good news of happiness" (Isaiah 52:7 ESV) and want it for themselves.

"To be truly happy—a man must have sources of gladness which are not dependent on anything in this world...Tell me not of your happiness, if it daily hangs on the uncertainties of earth."

J.C. Ryle

DAY 197

Against you, you only, have I sinned and done
what is evil in your sight;
so you are right in your verdict and
justified when you judge.

PSALM 51:4

It's a characteristic of evil people to think they're not evil. When we fail to see the truth that we've sinned against God above all—the One who has maximum worthiness—then no matter how badly we feel about what we've done to others, we will inevitably minimize our sin, and thereby minimize the redemptive work of Christ. Charles Spurgeon put it this way: "Too many think lightly of sin, and therefore think lightly of the Saviour."

There is great freedom in admitting our evil so we can fully experience the glorious, joyful, and gracious forgiveness of Jesus.

"My sin, oh, the bliss of this glorious thought!
My sin, not in part but the whole,
Is nailed to the cross, and I bear it no more,
Praise the Lord, praise the Lord, O my soul!"

Horatio Spafford

DAY 198

[The seraphim] were calling to one another:
"Holy, holy, holy is the Lord Almighty;
the whole earth is full of his glory."

Isaiah 6:3

A pastor wrote that we must see all other attributes of God in light of, and subordinate to, his love. But if love were God's predominant characteristic, wouldn't we expect the seraphim to cry, "Love, love, love is the Lord Almighty"?

Though he certainly could have, when Peter preached the gospel in Acts 3, he didn't refer to Jesus as "the Loving One" but "the Holy and Righteous One" (Acts 3:14).

Obviously Scripture affirms that Jesus is loving, and love is a vital attribute of God (1 John 4:8). But if love—at least as most people understand it—were the only attribute of God, then his holiness and wrath would have no place. Jesus is not only love, he is light and truth and life.

"We worship a God who is love; we do not worship love as our God."

Kevin DeYoung

DAY 199

But our citizenship is in heaven. And we eagerly await a Savior from there, the Lord Jesus Christ, who, by the power that enables him to bring everything under his control, will transform our lowly bodies so that they will be like his glorious body.

PHILIPPIANS 3:20-21

When we think of Heaven as unearthly, our present lives seem unspiritual, as if they don't matter. When we grasp the truth of the doctrines of creation, redemption, resurrection, and the New Earth, our present lives take on greater importance, infusing us with purpose.

Understanding Heaven doesn't just tell us *what* to do, but *why*. What God tells us about our future lives enables us to interpret our past and serve him in our present.

"When the followers of Christ lose their interest in heaven they will no longer be happy Christians, and...cannot be a powerful force in a sad and sinful world."

A.W. Tozer

DAY 200

I heard a voice thunder from the Throne: "Look! Look! God has moved into the neighborhood, making his home with men and women! They're his people, he's their God."

Revelation 21:3, *The Message*

When Christ-followers die, they go to live with God in his place. But the ultimate promise is even greater—that *God will come down to live with us in our place*, on the New Earth. The eventual Heaven will not be "us with God" but "God with us."

The typical view of Heaven, as a disembodied state, obscures the far richer biblical truth: God promises us eternal life. We'll say a final goodbye to sin and suffering and will be far more capable of true worship, friendship, love, discovery, work, play, and happiness than we've ever been.

"The only thing redemption adds that is not included in the creation is the remedy for sin...Grace *restores* nature, making it whole once more."

Albert Wolters

CONCLUSION

Truth at the Core of Our Worldview

Universities greatly influence the trajectory of their cultures since they are the training centers for future business, political, and media leaders. All of us are ultimately affected by what's taught and embraced as truth on the college campus.

University students were once known as truth-seekers. But now minds are so "open," most don't think critically.

Consider a video posted by the Family Policy Institute of Washington. A mid-thirties, five-foot-nine white male interviewed American university students. He asked them what they would think if he told them he was a woman. They were mostly fine with that, just as they were when he told them he was Chinese.

He said, "What if I told you I'm seven years old?" While some admitted he didn't look seven years old, they said they thought it was fine for him to identify himself as that. Several had no problem with him enrolling in grade school as a seven-year-old.

Then he said, "What if I told you I'm six feet five inches

tall?" Some struggled a bit, but they were generally okay with him identifying himself that way. Who were they to judge? Sometimes the students paused before answering, obviously conflicted because they knew his claims were false, but couldn't say it. Their core values were tolerance, relativity, and the right for everyone to identify themselves however they wish. The latter values ultimately overrode the value of objective truth.

When a thirty-five-year-old, five-foot-nine white man can claim to be a seven-year-old, six-foot-five Chinese woman without fear of objection from university students who will one day lead the country, we're naïve to think that every corner of our society won't ultimately be infected by such a distorted view of truth.

In *The Closing of the American Mind*, Allan Bloom said, "There is one thing a professor can be absolutely certain of: almost every student entering the university believes, or says he believes, that truth is relative."

G.K. Chesterton said, "The object of opening the mind, as of opening the mouth, is to shut it again on something solid."

With all the emphasis on having an open mind to "truths," one would think that people's minds would at least be open to the claims of the Christian worldview. But in that regard most people are characterized not by open-mindedness but closed-mindedness.

It's fine today to say you're searching for truth. It's not fine to say you've found it—especially in Jesus Christ, as revealed in the Bible.

Evading Truth's Demands

The secular environment is not as hostile toward religious belief in general as it is toward Christianity in particular. The same people who have no openness to Christianity may regard themselves as spiritual seekers. Karma? Sure. Fate? Why not? Throw in Buddhism, New Age, or angel-guided living. It's a "have it your way" designer religion, ruled by our desire to be our own gods, setting our own standards, rewriting objective truth to fit our subjective preferences.

It brings to mind the old adage, "If you stand for nothing, you'll fall for anything."

Why is it okay to accept any silly thing we want but not okay to believe Scripture? Perhaps because if the Bible is true and we'll be held accountable to God, then we're in trouble. We don't want to hear there's a God who created us, says we are sinners, makes demands on our lives, and claims to be our Judge that we must answer to.

The Eclipse of Truth

Suppose a professor or inspirational speaker says, "What's important isn't finding the truth, it's searching for it." Try applying the same logic to your search for a job, a parking space, or a life preserver when you're drowning.

Or, "There's no such thing as truth." Is that a true statement? If so, then there *is* such a thing as truth. If the statement is true, it proves itself false. And if there's no such thing as truth, how's it possible to weigh and measure the merit of ours or anyone else's beliefs and choices?

Or, "Truth is whatever you believe, as long as you're sincere." Certainly, you can step off a building sincerely believing you won't fall. But gravity cares nothing about your sincerity. Even sincere people are often wrong, sometimes catastrophically so.

Or, "What's true for you is true for you, and what's true for me is true for me." So if we step off a roof at the same time, I'll fall because I believe in gravity, but you'll hover because you don't?

Doesn't being ethnically Chinese involve having certain markers in one's DNA? Doesn't being a woman entail any objective physical realities? Is the claim of being six feet five inches tall objectively measurable as either a truth or a falsehood?

At what point does truth lose all meaning and "tolerance"

and "acceptance" of self-evident untruths become sheer nonsense?

True Truth

In light of encroaching relativism, in the 1960s, Francis Schaeffer coined the term "true truth" to convey the idea of absolute truth that exists independently of human opinion. Schaeffer recognized that the word *truth* was losing its historic meaning.

Jesus said God's Word is truth (John 17:17). It's not prideful to believe what the Bible teaches, it's humble because we recognize that God knows better than do we or the confused voices of our culture.

Arrogance is when we're presumptuous enough to believe whatever suits our tastes and preferences and those of modern people who we imagine are smarter and cooler than they really are.

Dismissing Christ as mistaken and the Bible as irrelevant is prideful beyond description. "Whoever does not believe God has made him out to be a liar" (1 John 5:10). What could be more arrogant—or dangerous—than calling God a liar?

Even those who claim to believe the Bible can be notoriously selective. Augustine said, "If you believe what you like in the gospel, and reject what you don't like, it is not the gospel you believe, but yourself."

Christians who arbitrarily embrace some biblical truths and reject others are severely handicapped in representing Christ to a truth-starved world. Churches desperately need to focus on teaching people the "whole counsel" of Scripture (Acts 20:27 ESV). Who are we to pick and choose which truths we like and don't like when God's Word says, "The sum of your word is truth, and every one of your righteous rules endures forever" (Psalm 119:160 ESV)?

The Impact of Truth

Recognizing the reality of objective truth, "true truth," God's truth, is the key to the present and future of our culture, as well as that of every individual, family, church, and community. Why? Because what we believe about truth will inevitably affect our moral values and how we live.

Since Jesus said the truth will set us free, failing to believe and live by it will enslave us to error, sin, and self-destruction. This is why it's vital that we join David in saying, "Show me your ways, LORD, teach me your paths. Guide me in your truth and teach me" (Psalm 25:4-5).

As long as we trust our own subjective judgment that ebbs and flows with the current of our culture, we divorce ourselves from God's eternal and unchanging truth. Once our eyes are opened to the transcendent beauty and freedom of God's truth, we'll never be content with anything less.

More than we can imagine hangs in the balance concerning what is true and whether or not we believe it. May we look to Jesus who is the Truth. And may God in his mercy help us to embrace and live according to the life-giving truth he has given us—both for his glory and for our good.

WHAT NEXT?

You may wish to reread this book and meditate on or memorize the Scriptures at its core. You might want to share it with a friend or discuss it with a group. If you're not part of a community of believers who are learning the truths of God's Word, find a Christ-centered, Bible-teaching church. (If you need help locating one in your area, contact our ministry at info@epm.org and we will assist you.)

Here are other truth-related books you may find helpful:

- *No Place for Truth: Or Whatever Happened to Evangelical Theology?* David F. Wells
- *Reasonable Faith: Christian Truth and Apologetics*, William Lane Craig
- *Truth Matters: Confident Faith in a Confusing World*, Andreas Köstenberger, Darrell Bock, Josh Chatraw
- *Bible Doctrine: Essential Teachings of the Christian Faith*, Wayne Grudem (author), Jeff Purswell (editor)
- *Total Truth: Liberating Christianity from Its Cultural Captivity*, Nancy Pearcey

- *The Reason for God: Belief in an Age of Skepticism*, Timothy Keller
- *A World of Difference: Putting Christian Truth-Claims to the Worldview Test*, Kenneth Richard Samples
- *The Grace and Truth Paradox*, Randy Alcorn

I also recommend *The Truth Project,* a small group curriculum centered on cultivating a Christian worldview. See www.thetruthproject.org

Scripture Quotation Sources

You'll Also Want to Read *Grace* by Randy Alcorn

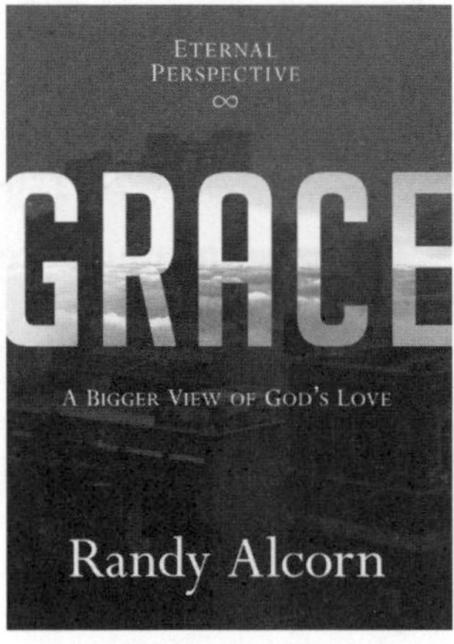

What would your life be like without the transforming power of God's grace? His grace gives comfort, strength, and encouragement when you face daily challenges both big and small. And best of all, this free gift of God's grace is available to everyone through a relationship with Jesus Christ.

Randy Alcorn, author of the bestselling book *Heaven*, offers daily meditations, scriptures, and inspirational quotes that will help you grasp more fully the grace God has lavished on you.

Come explore the riches of God's care for you, and fall more in love than ever before with the One who is full of grace and truth.

About the Author

Randy is the founder and director of Eternal Perspective Ministries, which began in 1990. Previously he served as a pastor for fourteen years. He has a bachelor of theology and a master of arts in biblical studies from Multnomah University and an honorary doctorate from Western Seminary in Portland, Oregon. He has taught on the adjunct faculties of both.

A *New York Times* bestselling author, Randy has written over fifty books, including *Happiness*, *Heaven* (over one million sold), *The Treasure Principle* (over two million sold), *If God Is Good*, and *Safely Home* (winner of the Gold Medallion award for fiction). His books have been translated into seventy languages and have sold ten million copies. Randy has written for many magazines including EPM's *Eternal Perspectives*. He blogs, is active daily on Facebook and Twitter, and has been a guest on more than eight hundred radio, television, and online programs.

Randy resides in Gresham, Oregon, with his wife, Nanci. They have two married daughters and are the proud grandparents of five grandsons. Randy enjoys hanging out with his family, biking, underwater photography, research, and reading.

Contact Eternal Perspective Ministries at www.epm.org or 39085 Pioneer Blvd., Suite 206, Sandy, OR 97055 or 503.668.5200. Follow Randy on Facebook: www.facebook.com/randyalcorn; Twitter: www.twitter.com/randyalcorn; and on his blog: www.epm.org/blog.